ENGAGE LEADERSHIP

Kickstart the Leadership Potential Within You!

NATALIE AMAN

DEDICATION

To my husband Riley, my best friend and love of my life! There is no one I would rather live this God adventure with! Also to my dear children Wesley and Annie it is my highest honor to be your mother!

CONTENTS

CHAPTER 1
START YOUR ENGINES
THE NECESSITY FOR ENGAGED LEADERS

I am not a fan of heights. By not a fan, I mean I was on a nice romantic hike with my husband, Riley, when a cliff to the right of me sent fear through my body. I stopped walking and started crawling up the mountain until eventually, I cheered Riley on as he finished the hike while I hid safely behind a big rock far below the summit!

Rewind fifteen years and you'll find me as a young teenager somehow being convinced by friends that it was a good idea to swim across the lake in order to climb a twenty-plus foot rock and jump off. They said, "It will be fun." Clearly, our definitions of fun are very different.

I mustered the courage to swim across the water, no problem. I boldly approached the rock and began to slowly climb up, not daring to look down below. Finally, I arose triumphantly on top of the herculean mountain I had built in my mind. I could taste the taste of sweet victory.

There was just one minor problem. Climbing up was the easy part. I now had to make my way to the edge of the rock and JUMP! Sheer panic filled my lungs. I'm sure Casper the Friendly Ghost would have looked tan next to me in that moment. But I stood on the edge of that rock, appearing courageous, yet looking for a way of escape. However, there was no escape, nor the possibility of climbing down. Being airlifted out was not a viable option either!

There I stood, fear running through my veins, saying a whole lot of silent prayer, wondering how I could have been so stupid as to listen to my friends. But peer pressure is real. And so I was faced with the reality of having only one clear option. Engage legs, propel forward, and jump off! Spoiler alert: I lived to tell the story, and I lived to say I have never done that again!

If we are honest, the thought of leading people can often feel a lot like hiking up a steep and dangerous mountain, and like jumping off the edge of a high cliff into deep water below. As a result, we find ourselves hesitating. We often wait for someone else to volunteer to lead and mobilize a group. We find every reason why the timing is not right, or why we are disqualified from taking the lead and stepping into the new role. Perhaps the idea of leadership sounds cool. We visualize our title on a business card, but when the opportunity presents itself, we're frozen with fear of climbing new heights and paralyzed by the thought of taking the plunge.

I would like to propose that there is only one way to start leading! Wait for it... You just have to start!

Every great leader throughout history had a moment when they engaged, took the risk, and jumped in with both feet.

I have one core mission in this book: That you would climb to the high rock, jump off of it, take the plunge, and dive into the deep part of the water. Are you catching my drift?

My desire is that wherever you are in your leadership journey, you would take that next step to engage in a fresh way, and that you would accept the leadership mission God has set before you.

Each one of us is presented with the same number of hours in a day, days in a week, and weeks in a year. Yet, only you can choose how you will engage each moment and embrace the God-given call to lead.

Most people can see the need for leaders to emerge in the needy world around us, but we must individually determine to step into being part of the fulfillment of that need.

Throughout history, change has happened through the simple courage of one person at one moment in time; a person who was willing to step out of the crowd and take their place to lead the crowd!

More than Hypothetical

There are some things you don't want to be the beta test for. I, for one, don't want to be the guinea pig patient for a first-time surgeon, or be a passenger on the maiden voyage of an airline pilot. I don't care how good of a score they achieved on their flight simulator, I'll wait a few years!

If I am going to take the plunge of engaging in a life of leadership, I don't want a bunch of hypothetical ideas or unproven methods. I want to see real-life evidence of leaders before me who engaged in this great mission of leadership, who paid the price, and saw the fruit of transformation!

This is one reason I love the Bible. In it, God has laid out the real-life accounts of men and women who paved the way in leadership. We recognize their scars, fears, questions, failures, and successes. 1 Corinthians 10:11 tells us; *"Now these things happened to them as an example, but they were written down for our instruction, on whom the end of the ages has come."*

One of the most inspiring leaders in my life is someone who, this side of eternity, I will never get to meet. But through the beautiful Word of God, I can get an insider's look at his leadership and wisdom.

Who is this influential leader?
Nehemiah!

The following are just a few highlights of Nehemiah's leadership successes. He would:

- Restore and rebuild the wall in Jerusalem in an astonishing 52 days.
- Rally and unite a varied group of people to help him accomplish this mission.
- Lead through great opposition.
- Govern the land for twelve years.

The book of Nehemiah is like having a personal leadership journal and play-by- play book based on the powerful leadership expeditions that God used Nehemiah for. Trends change, technology is rapidly moving, but proven leadership truths are timeless. As we journey through this book, we will look at some of the brilliant leadership insights from the life of Nehemiah.

The life and leadership of Nehemiah are not hype or without struggle. Rather, we see a man who faced real obstacles, and at times, seemingly impossible feats that lay ahead of him. And yet, we see a man who grabbed the bull by the horns, engaged his leadership, and saw the near impossible become a reality!

Twenty Seconds of Insane Courage

One of my husband's and my favorite movies is called "We Bought a Zoo." The main character, Benjamin Mee, played by Matt Damon, recounts a story to his kids about when he first met his late wife. Ben tells how he walked past the window of a small cafe and saw a beautiful woman who was a complete stranger to him. When he saw her, he stopped in his tracks. Then he did something absolutely crazy! He walked into that cafe and talked to this strange woman who would later become his wife and mother of his children.

He tells his children these words: *"You know, sometimes all you need is 20 seconds of insane courage, just literally 20 seconds of embarrassing bravery, and I promise you something great will come of it."*

Riley and I often quote those words. In fact, that quote has become a great encouragement to propel us forward and engage our leadership potential.

There will always be a million excuses or reasons why we shouldn't lead. There will consistently be a persistent whisper telling you why you aren't qualified to build the wall. Maybe you have led "all in" before but at some point in the journey, you got stuck or paralyzed by fear and/or disappointment. Yet, what if today was the day you kissed those excuses goodbye? What if today was the day you leaned in and stepped forward into the God-sized mission He has set before you?

Perhaps all you need, my friend, is twenty seconds of insane courage. I promise you, something great will come of it!

It's time to engage our leadership like never before!

CHAPTER 2
KILL THE MICROWAVE

Patience is a virtue. It's just that it's a virtue I am still in great need of.

I'm the queen of "This Should Have Happened Five Minutes Ago!" I am the leader who sets timers in team meetings to make sure we are staying on track. And I confess, I've even been known to set sixty-second timers in a small group to make sure people were moving through their sharing time in an efficient manner. I want the heart-to-heart dialogue, just maybe a bit sped up! (I can feel your judgment!)

Once I know where I'm going, I don't want to dilly dally. Let's get on the road and get moving. Road trips with Riley and I are a blast, I promise!

I have learned one thing, though, when it comes to leadership and engaging in the mission of God. God is not on my timeline, and His training ground looks very different than one crafted by any human.

Hebrews 6:12b tells us, "... *but imitators of those who through faith and patience inherit the promises.*"

God's development plan, which is to teach us to obtain His promises, is a one-two punch of Faith and Patience.

Throughout the Bible, when God wanted to mightily use and develop a leader, that potential leader was often placed on the "slow track" of development. It appears that when God identified a leader to be pulled from the crowd, He then sent them to the back of the line.

A Few Examples of Slow Track Development Include:

- At seventy-five years old, Abraham responds to the call of God to leave Haran, and receives the promise that he would be a blessing and be fruitful. Twenty five years later, Abraham receives the promised son -- at the prime age of one hundred! Ten years into the waiting, God reassures Abraham that the promise was still coming! Nothing about this tells me that God was in a rush to fulfill His promise.

- Moses has a miraculous launch into the world, is raised forty years in the palace of Pharaoh, and has an epic superhero moment of wanting to help his fellow Israelites. Moses then goes into the wilderness for forty more years of schooling and development. In reality, God gave Moses eighty years of education to engage him for forty years of leading his people!

- David spends the first seventeen years or so of his life faithfully serving his father as a shepherd boy. Then God throws this awesome anointing party and declares that the youngest brother of eight, the shepherd boy and cheese deliverer, would now be KING of God's people. It seems that was the moment to cue the band and drop the confetti. Nope. David then goes into intense training for the next 13 years, which includes slaying giants, warring, serving, dodging spears, betrayal, hiding, cave dwelling, and character development. Only after all that could David step into the beginning phase of his kingship.

- Jesus spends thirty seemingly quiet years to the outside world. These three decades of development would propel Him into three and a half years of resolute purposeful ministry. Just as Jesus comes on the scene, is baptized, and publicly applauded by the Father, He is sent into the wilderness by the Spirit to be tempted for forty days. This seems like the time to get the news out and launch His public campaign, but instead, more development is happening in the wilderness!

We could go on and on through the Bible and see leaders who were identified and then forged in the training arena of faith and patience. Jacob, Joseph, Joshua, Esther, John the Baptist, and the Apostle Paul, just to name a few.

Overnight Success is the Product of Over-The-Years Faithfulness

I'm a Millennial. There, I said it.

I am a child of Amazon Prime two-day delivery. Fast-casual dining is my friend. I mobile order my food and watch the progress bar to make sure the restaurateurs and delivery drivers hit their stated timeframe. I have grown up with Google readily available to answer any question I have at every waking moment.

I have also grown up in a world that can easily create an illusion that anyone can be an overnight success. If you post a funny enough video, you may be the next Internet sensation. If enough people see my fifteen seconds of karaoke fame on social media, I could be touring the world and standing on a platform of instant stardom.

We laugh. We shrug this off. But in reality, the instant, at-our-fingers, digital age has deeply affected how we engage in the process of leadership development.

When we are in the trenches of life and leadership development, it can feel like something is wrong with us because it looks like everyone around us has achieved instant success. It appears that everyone else is living out their idyllic best self for the whole world to see.

This wrong view can not only cause us anguish, it can also lead us astray. When we see someone who has truly paid the price to be developed and is now walking in success, we prefer to ignore their example in pursuit of the more "efficient" easy route.

Big mistake. The truth is, this so-called overnight success is almost always the product of over-the-years faithfulness.

Let me say that one more time. Overnight success is almost always the product of over-the-years faithfulness.

Leaders who build something that outlasts them and changes the world around them are those who are developed in the school of Faith and Patience year after year.

My father-in-law was raised on a hazelnut farm, working from an early age with his brothers. Now, they have taken that farm far beyond what anyone could have imagined. Every fall there are specific days when the hazelnut trees release the harvest. During those September days, my father-in-law and his crew work long days with great joy as they bring in an abundant harvest. Most people observing harvest days on the hazelnut farm would think, "I could do that. I have what it takes to bring in the harvest. It's a piece of cake!" The harvest looks like an overnight success. It looks like the brothers must have just gotten lucky.

Yet, I have been around during the cold, rainy season, when the orchards have lost their beauty. My father-in-law faithfully takes care of the trees. I have watched him and his brothers scheme to find new patches of land to sow new trees, knowing that it will take years before the saplings ever give back fruit to be consumed. I have seen how in the long summer days filled with heat and toilsome work, my father-in-law faithfully nurtures and waters every tree. The sweet victory of the September harvest is the product of grueling work sown over the other eleven months.

Where Did They Learn That?

We can read about the leadership of Nehemiah and think he was simply in the right place at the right time. We might even conclude that he happened to fall into a leader's paradise and optimized on his investment. Wrong.

Nehemiah accomplished a miraculous feat of building the wall of Jerusalem in fifty two days because Nehemiah was being forged for decades prior to that.

Remember, Nehemiah spent his entire life living in a land that was not his own. He grew up hearing about his people, the temple that once stood gloriously, and the miracles of the one true God. He lived in a foreign land among a foreign people, far from the beauty of that which his ancestors once enjoyed.

Nehemiah also knew the prophetic words declared almost 150 years prior by the prophet, as stated in Jeremiah 29:4-7, 10-11 (ESV):

"Thus says the LORD of hosts, the God of Israel, to all the exiles whom I have sent into exile from Jerusalem to Babylon: Build houses and live in them; plant gardens and eat their produce. Take wives and have sons and daughters; take wives for your sons, and give your daughters in marriage, that they may bear sons and daughters; multiply there, and do not decrease. **But seek the welfare of the city where I have sent you into exile, and pray to the LORD on its behalf, for in its welfare you will find your welfare."***

"For thus says the LORD: **When seventy years are completed for Babylon, I will visit you, and I will fulfill to you my promise and bring you back to this place.** *For I know the plans I have for you, declares the LORD, plans for welfare and not for evil, to give you a future and a hope."*

Here in a land far, far away from home, we find Nehemiah fulfilling the words that had been prophesied by the Prophet Jeremiah.

Here in the fortress of Susa, Nehemiah is seeking the welfare of this city and he is serving the king faithfully. He is seeking the welfare of this place of exile, and because of that, Nehemiah is about to see that God will cause him to see fruitfulness in his own land.

The leadership development of Nehemiah didn't begin when he heard the news about the sad state of the city of God, or as he set out on the long journey to Jerusalem.

This process had started decades earlier before we ever knew who Nehemiah was.

This exiled Jewish boy had gone through seasons of serving in the king's palace. In the unseen moments Nehemiah was found faithful, trustworthy, and excellent.

When we finally come into Nehemiah's story, he is cupbearer to the king. Now, lest you think this is a step up from a busboy at your favorite restaurant, being cupbearer is one of the most significant positions in the entire kingdom.

The Cupbearer Required Some Key Job Qualifications on their Resume. Here are Three Main Ones:

- **Courageous-** The life of the king rested in the cupbearer's hands. He would taste the wine in front of the king to make sure it was free of poison. Every single day Nehemiah risked his own life for the sake of the king. He courageously endangered his own life to protect the one he served.

- **Completely trustworthy-** Few people were allowed in close proximity to the king. Cupbearers were among those few. They were not only found trustworthy with preserving the life of the king, but were trusted with royal secrets and situations that required silence and complete loyalty.

- **Full of discretion and wisdom-** The cupbearer had to be discreet in his interactions with the king and in what he heard within the walls of the palace. The cupbearer also had to be wise and respond appropriately when dealing with the whims and the moods of the king.

How Nehemiah found himself in this place of great honor, we don't get the privilege of knowing, but we do know that he was held in high favor with the king. We also know that Nehemiah's faithfulness in that season became the foundation God used for Nehemiah to be favored in the eyes of the king, which allowed him to fulfill the great mission that lay before him.

Through observation and deductive reasoning, we see that in the royal palace of a foreign people,God was developing a mighty leader for His purposes. In what appears to be a long delay, the mighty hand of God was upon Nehemiah forming the strength and wisdom necessary for him to accomplish the mission without being crushed by it.

Through the often mundane daily tasks that Nehemiah was doing, he was listening in on royal conversations, seeing a king and his leaders lead, observing the inner workings of leadership and authority.

Nehemiah observed how the king desired to be approached. He became intimate with the habits and behaviors of the king, which enabled him to know the timing that was just right to make monumental requests of the king. When the right time came for Nehemiah to make the "BIG ASK" of the king, he had already been prepared long before this.

The outside world saw a cupbearer serving a king faithfully. But the reality was that God was forming a world-renowned leader and surrounding him with favor in the most unlikely place!

Delayed Development is the Result of Failing to Develop During the Delay

Delay can be the graveyard of a leader or it can be the launching pad for a lifetime of effective fruitfulness. How you spend time in the midst of delay determines the fruit on the other side of it.

You can sit in delay and waste that time, or you can observe and strategize during the delay. You can use your energy to identify the tools of development that are available to you in that difficult season.

Delay in leadership is often like the stage of "foundation formation" in our lives. Nothing is very glamorous about the foundation laying season in a building project. Most people aren't walking around saying, "Do you see the way that beautiful concrete is drying? Wow, I've seen foundations, but man, that is one incredible slab of concrete!"

Yet, when it comes time to build on top of that foundation, people begin to care deeply. They are thankful that exact measurements were made. Gratitude fills their heart to know that the necessary time was given to put the precise forms in place to allow the concrete to be molded as it was intended.

The season of delay in leadership is more about preparing you for what you are planning to build. It's about forming the needed strength and skills for that which is yet to come. I would love to say that leadership development is like a ladder that, once you've passed one rung, you never have to face it again. But it is simply not so. Seasons of delay will happen at different times throughout your leadership journey, and will require you to lay fresh foundations for that which is to come!

In my seasons of delay, I have laid the foundation for skills I will cultivate in my leadership, I am identifying the values that actually matter, I am building the muscles of endurance and faithfulness, and so much more.

There are a Few Practical Tools We Can Take Hold of from Nehemiah's Season in the King's Palace:

1. **Develop where you are**- We don't get to choose where or when God starts the development process. However, we can choose to say yes or no to that process. Our yes moves us forward. Every no gets us stuck. Nehemiah didn't choose to be born as an exile, nor did he choose his position in the king's palace, but he did decide to dive headfirst into the leadership waters as an exile and cupbearer in the palace.

   Engaged leaders see the world around them like a jungle gym for their development. They see the disadvantages, trials, and delay as opportunities to make them stronger, more adaptable leaders! I don't know where you find yourself currently, but I would challenge you to accept where you are and start developing smack dab in the middle of the here and now!

2. **Make "here" a success-** Your desire to go and build will never be a true success until you learn to make the here and now a success. Engaged leaders are not waiting for some day but determine that even in the midst of the unknown they will be fully invested. Nehemiah made wherever he was a success. He served faithfully in the land of exile and therefore was able to make the land of his mission a success as well. God honors the leader who is faithful with what he has been entrusted in the place he has been entrusted with it.

Our job as engaged leaders is to build what's in front of us where we are, not daydream about doing something someday, somewhere else. We should leave a trail of successes behind us at the end of our lives. We have the opportunity to leave a legacy that shows that in every season we were present and engaged in making the here and now a success!

3. **Don't rush the timing-** No matter how long you stare at the clock or the calendar, time won't speed up. We don't choose the timing or the season of development, but we do get to choose to embrace it and nurture it. Then we can be sure that the seeds of development will bring forth fruit in its perfect and due time. But no, it cannot be rushed. There is a lot to glean from the wise words King Solomon wrote in Ecclesiastes 3:13 (ESV): *"For everything there is a season, and a time for every matter under heaven:"*

Great strength is developed in the leader who peacefully walks out their season of waiting, and with joy, endures through the long, grueling days of development. Even after Nehemiah heard the news about the state of the Jerusalem wall, he did not rush the timing. Instead, he waited four months for the opportune time to speak to the King.

Let it Simmer

My mother is Sicilian and my brothers and I all proudly embrace every ounce of blood that comes from that Sicilian heritage.

By embracing it, I mean we are all certifiable Italian food snobs. We feel that having even twenty-five percent of that "Italian amore" running through our veins gives us the license to judge the quality of any red sauce that crosses our lips.

Disclaimer: I apologize in advance if I offend your food-eating choices over the next few paragraphs!

If you walk into my parent's home with a clear jar of store-bought marinara sauce, you may as well have slapped my mother across the face. And you just might hear my mother repeating the words of my late Sicilian Papa: "Ish…" Trust me, you do not want to hear the word "Ish" when it comes to your cooking!

We take our red sauce very seriously. We have one particular sauce that has been passed down in the family and it has two names.

First, we call it long sauce. The second name is…

L-I-Q-U-I-D G-O-L-D!

Yes, you heard me correctly! Liquid Gold. It's precious. It's like a treasure. So my mother has trained me and each of my sisters in-law, and now my oldest niece, Evie, how to make long sauce from scratch, starting with the beginning stage.

This, my friends, is an all-day process.

We first create the flavors, using only the highest quality herbs and spices. We then hand roll trays and trays of meatballs, spare ribs, and sausage. Each ingredient is intentionally layered in at the appropriate time. Multiple roasters are filled with this precious commodity as it simmers away for hours. Oh, if you could only smell the most glorious aroma as this culinary delicacy cooks throughout the day. And it's with giddy anticipation that the whole family awaits the moment we get to gather around the table and feast!

After hours of love and labor, focused attention, and careful crafting, the family and our lucky guests enjoy the fruit of this long-awaited sauce. Somehow, knowing the sacrifice that went into its development makes each bite tastier, more meaningful, and appreciated.

Time to Kill the Microwave

As leaders, we have a choice. We can engage the long and often slow process of development that in the end produces a well seasoned and strong leader. Or, we can follow the cultural patterns of instant gratification, wanting instant success, and putting untested and under-developed leaders into service too soon.

You can get your sauce out of a jar and heat it in the microwave, but you can't pretend that it tastes as good as the Liquid Gold long sauce. And trust me, when you taste the fruit of leadership that has been lovingly developed for the long haul, you'll never go back to the untested imitation of instant success.

Anything worth building is worth the effort and hard work it requires. A God-sized vision and mission is worth giving your whole life for. And it is worth the investment of time because the slow process of preparation results in a lifetime of fruit.

Perhaps it's time to pull out the dutch oven and put the microwave in the garage for a bit. In this beautiful process of preparation, God is crafting and forming you as a leader who will last, and will one day gather around, and with deep gratitude enjoy the fruit of your perseverance and faithfulness.

- INNOVATE-

| in·no·vate |

Phase 1

Innovation 1: a new idea, method, or device:

2: the introduction of something new.

Innovate: to make changes: do something in a new way.

There's a moment when things begin to shift, when something begins to stir in the heart and mind of a growing leader, and they begin to dream about what could be. This is Phase 1 of engaged leadership, also referred to as the "Innovate" phase.

In the Innovate phase, a vision begins to formulate in the mind of a leader. These thoughts, new ideas, and potential changes then get translated onto the whiteboard. It's the time when leaders begin to ask themselves and their team members questions such as:

- "What if we tried something we never tried before?"
- "Could we be the answer to this need around us?"
- "What if we built something that no one else is building?"
- "What changes must be made in order to move forward?"

The list of questions could go on and on because there is no limit to the creativity during the Innovate phase. As a result, there's a new confidence being developed that allows leaders at all levels to believe they can accomplish a vision far bigger than they ever imagined.

Meanwhile, the phase of innovation establishes a blueprint for others to rally behind and help the leader accomplish their goals! It is in the stage of innovation that the vision begins to find clarity and direction so it can later be communicated to the team. Without the stage of innovation, you have no mission or vision for the team to gather around. This phase is vital in the ultimate success of reaching the stated goal. As others have wisely said, "You get out of it what you put into it!" If you will give energy to effective innovation, it will set you up to later motivate and activate those around you to accomplish something that perhaps has never been done before!

CHAPTER 3

THE MOMENT THAT CHANGES EVERYTHING

I had just finished preaching for the fourth time in one weekend, first at a retreat and then for a church in California. I had one last message to share that evening with a group of leaders.

I found myself in the summer heat with my husband and some friends from where I was ministering, and they were taking us to get their famous "slushies!" They adamantly informed us that their slushies were better than Slurpees. What a bold claim! I enjoyed those few hours with my husband and friends, and loved getting to cool off with the famous refreshing beverages. I thought I was nearing the end of a fruitful time of ministry, leadership, and fellowship. Little did I know that I was about to experience a moment that would change everything.

That evening I met with a small group of about twenty-five or thirty core leaders from the church. The pastor had asked me to share so I prepared some leadership thoughts from the life of Nehemiah and shared them with the group. Afterward, they began to ask questions about leadership, structures, systems, challenges, and more. For about forty-five minutes I engaged this group by sharing leadership principles, as well as sharing my personal thoughts and own experiences in leading people. As I answered, it dawned on me that I was in my element, enjoying every minute of that moment. The words just flowed out of me. Little did I know that I would be marked like never before after this informal leadership training time.

I finished the session and it hit me like a ton of bricks. For the first time in my life I had a sense of my purpose, and I said to myself "This is why I am on planet earth." "I get it, this is why I am the way I am." "I was made for this!"

I had preached hundreds of times. I had sat in small and large groups of leaders. I had built and led teams of leaders.

Yet, here in a small room of leaders, God ignited a flame on the inside of my heart and whispered my "White Hot Why!" By the way, a White Hot Why is a leadership term that describes having a purpose or it answers the question why you're willing to do whatever it takes to make something happen.

I was nearly twelve years into full-time leadership and ministry when I got my first real clue to the core meaning of my life. That revelation didn't happen very fast, but when it did, it was very powerful.

Suddenly, so much of my life, passions, and wrestlings made sense.

I remember sharing this revelation with my husband when I got home. I said something like, "I think I know why I am on planet earth!" I explained how something in me came alive as I was answering their questions with passion and authority. And while I didn't know exactly what I was going to do with this personal life-changing moment, I knew that it was something I couldn't ignore and that I must give my life to. It was something I had to lean into!

C.S Lewis said, "This moment contains all moments."

There are moments in our lives when all of our prior experiences suddenly make sense, and the revelation of the present moment allows our future to make sense.

This was not just any moment. This was a moment that changed everything!

A series of Fortunate Events

Many leaders can look back at key moments that changed their lives and trajectories, moments when life made sense and they recognized a piece of the mission God had given them.

It is possible to be actively leading, actively building, but not have a "White Hot Why." You can have success around you, but not yet be engaged in the full mission God created you for.

You can't really plan this moment of eye-opening awareness to the mission. You can't fabricate a lasting passion. But you can be ready to respond when the moment that changes everything happens.

Leadership is a series of "hurry up and wait" moments. We are often faced with a lot of micro-moments that don't feel monumental at the time, but when we look in reverse we see how they were setting us up for the moment when we finally moved to a whole new level.

Sometimes, these bite-sized moments equip us with the tools we need for the future. Other times, in the series of small moments, we can easily miss the clues they are giving. We don't realize that every moment actually adds fuel to the fire of our leadership and mission, until finally, our hearts are ablaze and we must lean "all in" to the mission at hand!

Something Has to Change

For Nehemiah, the moment that changed everything came on a seemingly ordinary day. Nehemiah's brother, Hanani, and some men from Judah were visiting. With a simple question, Nehemiah's whole world would be flipped upside down.

Nehemiah asked how the Jews who escaped the exile were doing, and how the city of Jerusalem was. The answers to these two questions were so troubling to Nehemiah that he would never be the same again.

This moment is revealed in Nehemiah 1:3-4. *"And they said to me, "The remnant there in the province who had survived the exile is in great trouble and shame. The wall of Jerusalem is broken down, and its gates are destroyed by fire." As soon as I heard these words I sat down and wept and mourned for days, and I continued fasting and praying before the God of heaven.* (ESV)

"As soon as I heard these words…"

Those words birthed a fire. Those words stirred Nehemiah to become personally invested in the restoration of the broken wall, and the well being of the troubled people.

Nehemiah could never un-hear those words.

I wonder how many times in the twelve years Nehemiah was governor of Jerusalem he closed his eyes and remembered the one single encounter that ignited his passion to lead his people. If I were Nehemiah, I would have thought a lot about that!

For years in the palace, and in his position as cupbearer to the Persian king, Nehemiah was a faithful leader and a good steward of what was entrusted to him. But in a single moment, he knew something had to change, and it was up to him to make sure that it did!

I can't tell you how many times as a leader I have gone back to those significant moments where a passion was ignited or vision was received. As I remember those moments, they fuel me for the task at hand. When was the last time you heard something or saw a need and it gripped you in an unshakeable way? When was the last time you felt called to do something new or to make a major change? To Innovate?

Whatever you do, do not ignore those key moments in your life and in your role as a leader. Remember those times when your heart was gripped with a problem and you knew that the solution was your responsibility. Dust off those places of passion, or lean into that fresh fire that's igniting and begin to give energy to doing something about what's right in front of you right now!

Here are a Few Practical Tools to Recognize and Grab Hold of Pivotal Leadership Moments:

- **Listen to the unspoken opportunity in the need-** Experienced leaders learn to read between the lines. They hear the call to action when others just hear the need at hand. Many people would have heard what Nehemiah heard about the broken wall and the plight of the people and thought, "Wow, that's too bad." "I really hope it gets better soon." Yet

Nehemiah heard a personal call for him to arise and become an answer to the dire need at hand. We must lean in intentionally as leaders to listen for the leadership opportunity, not just the mountains of impossibility. Next time you ask a question, listen for the opportunity inside the answer.

- **Make it personal**- Throughout history, the actions and decisions of some of the greatest leaders reveal a common thread in their leadership - their mission was personal. They dove headfirst into something that mattered, and they were willing to run into the fire even if it cost them everything. The moment Nehemiah heard "these words," it became personal to him. This was not a fight for someone else to win, it was now his fight. Nehemiah immediately became sad. He wept, mourned, fasted, prayed, and later we discovered that he was planning! I love watching a leader in a meeting come alive and fight to see something happen for their team! There's a glimmer of fire in their eyes that says, "This is personal, this matters to me!" People will follow a leader who has made the mission personal and are willing to go all in to accomplish it.

- **Make it happen-** Engaged leaders pre-determine that they will make it happen before they figure out how they will make it happen. When you get a vision bigger than yourself, start running towards the mission and formulate a plan as you go. I believe something shifted in Nehemiah when he heard the words that changed everything, and I believe he knew immediately that he would be a major part of the solution. All he had left to do was decide on a plan and then move forward with that plan. He had grit. Leaders with grit, who commit to summiting the mountain one way or another, will accomplish the mission even if it's nearly impossible and costs everything. Passion fuels these leaders and brings about the ultimate plan.

So what is it? What is your "White Hot Why?"

What is that passion burning in your heart? What task or project is holding on and won't let go? What is it that you know you have to do something about?

The world has more than enough critics. There are plenty of backseat drivers and armchair quarterbacks talking about the dire need and what everyone else should do.

What is needed now, and will be needed tomorrow, are leaders who burn with an unquenchable passion to make a difference. The world needs leaders who will give their lives to building something that will far outlive them, and who will raise up an army to accomplish today's mission and be an example to future leaders.

The Following are Three Action Steps to Make Sure This Moment Turns into Something Powerful

1. Write it down- There is tremendous power in the simple act of writing down your goals. A study was done with a few hundred people and it found that the likelihood of achieving goals went up by forty-two percent when they were written down on paper or on a device. So, stop right now and write your "White Hot Why." Write down the dreams that are stirring in your heart, even if they are small and missing some details. Then write a list of goals that will help you move forward.

2. Share it with someone- Now go tell one intentional person about the goals you wrote down. It's amazing how powerful it is to invite someone into your vision who can encourage you in the journey and support your vision as it comes to life. There is something freeing about the act of sharing. And it's good to have accountability. We all need someone to challenge us as we pursue our dream, and someone who will call us out in order to make sure we're making it happen. Maybe you need to pull your phone out right now and text that person and ask them if you can buy them coffee and share something that's burning in your heart!

3. Start today- There is no time like the present. You may not be able to do everything today, but you can do something today. Don't wait until Monday, next month, or a new season. Make a goal to take one step in putting the ball into play. Maybe it's as simple as reading a book that will educate you more in achieving the mission. Perhaps it's setting a timer that reminds you to stop and pray about the vision, or it could be giving fifteen minutes a day towards making progress in reaching your goal. Put this book down right now and get started! Do something. Do one thing. Then please come back and finish this book!

The movie Braveheart is a great example of how a leader who is infused with passion can achieve extraordinary things. (Don't worry, you don't need to wear a skirt and paint your face blue to show your leadership passion.) The movie recounts the story of a thirteenth-century Scottish hero by the name of William Wallace. Wallace's picture could be alongside the definition of the word "passion." The movie shows how this Scottish man fearlessly rallies and leads a group of Scottish warriors.

A famous line from the movie is Wallace declaring, *"Every man dies. Not every man really lives."* Wallace would in fact give his life for the sake of his mission, but not before really living.

Leader. May we not coast through life numb to the needs around us. May we not settle for anything less than discovering our calling, catching a God-sized vision, and giving our lives to seeing it come forth.

This is your moment to really live, to really build, and to give yourself in a fresh way to something that truly matters.

Perhaps as you read these words, God could be igniting a spark of passion in your heart. Is this that moment that changes everything?

CHAPTER 4

THE WAR ROOM!

"Nothing of eternal significance happens apart from prayer." I heard those gripping words as I sat in a room with a small group of college students. The man who made that statement spoke with such sincerity and conviction, it was clear to me that he was a man who had lived out that truth. He was a missionary who had given his life to reaching the people in the Republic of Ireland. He knew what it was like to be in an environment that unless God miraculously showed up, and stirred the hearts of the hearers, his labor was in vain.

This humble pastor had given his life to praying for a divine move of God and being positioned to engage in a move of God. As he continued to share with us, he declared, *"We walk where people have prayed and one day people will walk where I pray."*

Now, decades after he arrived to give his life to reaching a nation with the love of Jesus, multiple churches have been started and are now led by the Irish themselves. The land that St. Patrick had once prayed over, was a land that Pastor Gary Davidson became an answered prayer to. And now, there are others walking in that land as answers to the prayers that Pastor Gary prayed!

The engaged leader doesn't run to prayer as their last resort, but rather lives from the place of prayer in every season of their life.

The war room of a leader is not the place of strategy or good ideas. The war room of a leader is the place of prayer!

We often hear about the amazing leadership wisdom of Nehemiah, and about his courage to face the opposition head on. Yet, when you look at the life of Nehemiah, you can't help but recognize that he was always praying, always devoted, and completely dependent on God.

Nehemiah wasn't just a man who prayed, he was a man of prayer. For example, when Nehemiah receives news about the state of Jerusalem and its broken walls, he immediately turns his heart to the Lord in prayer and fasting.

Part of Nehemiah's first recorded prayer is found in Nehemiah 1:6 when he declares, *"Let your ear be attentive and your eyes open, to hear the prayer of your servant that I now pray before you day and night for the people of Israel your servants..." (ESV)*

Nehemiah then proceeds to end this same prayer in verse 11 with, *"O Lord, let your ear be attentive to the prayer of your servant, and to the prayer of your servants who delight to fear your name, and give success to your servant today, and grant him mercy in the sight of this man..."*

This is a cry of a leader who understands that even the most well-developed strategy is nothing compared to the divine intervention of God's power.

The book of Nehemiah records nine different times Nehemiah prayed. It is very evident that Nehemiah lived a lifestyle of prayer and it infused every element of his leadership. He prayed publicly, in distress, in times of needed wisdom, in leading the people, and in the face of the taunts of the enemies, just to name a few.

George Mueller was a leader who lived as an example of someone who lived out of the war room of prayer and engaged in being a leader who actively built. He modeled a life of absolute dependence on God to provide for him and the thousands of orphans he would end up caring for. In an article by desiringgod.org we get a small glimpse of what God did through the life of Mr. Mueller.

"He built five large orphan houses and cared for 10,024 orphans in his life. When he started in 1834 there were accommodations for 3,600 orphans in

all of England and twice that many children under eight were in prison. One of the great effects of Mueller's ministry was to inspire others so that "fifty years after Mr. Mueller began his work, at least one hundred thousand orphans were cared for in England alone." He did all this while he was preaching three times a week from 1830 to 1898, at least 10,000 times. And when he turned 70 he fulfilled a life-long dream of missionary work for the next 17 years until he was 87. He traveled to 42 countries, preaching on average of once a day, and addressing some three million people."

There is no way to accomplish the above feats apart from the divine help and working of God. This quote from George Mueller sums up the life of prayer and full dependence on God that he lived:

"I live in the spirit of prayer. I pray as I walk about, when I lie down and when I rise up. And the answers are always coming. Thousands and tens of thousands of times have my prayers been answered. When once I am persuaded that a thing is right and for the glory of God, I go on praying for it until the answer comes. George Mueller never gives up!"

Find Your Space

The work that God entrusts each of us with is of great importance, but absolutely impossible if He doesn't breathe life upon it. Therefore, our first priority as leaders is to carve out a time and a place to consistently seek the Lord in prayer.

The secret sauce of leadership in the life of believers is prayer. The world has many brilliant leaders, and there are millions of resources available at the click of a button to help build great systems and teams. Yet, all of this knowledge still leaves us lacking.

The Bible is filled with living examples of leaders whose first response was to seek the Lord in prayer. The greatest example of all was Jesus Himself. He modeled to us what it looked like to lead from a place of constant communion with the Father.

Jesus prayed all night before He called His team of leaders to join Him. He prayed first thing before making any appointments. Jesus showed us the true picture of what it means "to pray without ceasing" according to 1 Thessalonians 5:17

If we are going to truly lead out of this place of prayer, we must be intentional in how we build it into our daily lives and leadership programs.

1. **Make it Personal-** We can never lead others publicly where we have not first won privately. The public victory of a leader is often the fruit of private battles won in the personal time of prayer. We must prioritize personal time with Jesus in our everyday life.

2. **Make it Practical-** It's been said before that if you fail to plan, you are planning to fail. So plan on creating a lifestyle of

prayer, which requires leaders to make practical lifestyle choices. Three simple choices include:

- o **Have a Certain Time**- Establish a daily time to personally seek the Lord. I've heard of one leader who schedules a daily appointment with Jesus -- it's written on their Planner. It's really hard to justify canceling an appointment with Jesus.

- o **Have a Certain Place**- Where will you consistently meet with God in a time of prayer? Jesus would often withdraw to an isolated place to pray. The late Susanna Wesley would cover her head with her apron. Her kids all knew that was the sign that their mother was in her "certain place" of prayer and they better not mess with her!

- o **Have a Certain Plan**- Successful leaders show up to a meeting prepared with an agenda and a plan. Having clear focus and a plan during a time of prayer makes that moment so much more efficient and productive. There are many helpful resources intended to develop and focus our personal times of prayer! Having a plan can help us develop the tools to live a lifestyle of praying without ceasing.

3. **Make it Public-** The people we lead need to see us live lifestyles of prayer. The disciples saw Jesus modeling a life of

prayer "up close and personal," and it eventually led them to ask Jesus to teach them how to pray. Nehemiah modeled what it looked like to war in prayer. The teams we lead will always follow what we do, far more than what we say. Make sure that you are modeling prayer in the middle of all that you do!

Sometimes it's easy to begin the journey of leadership in the place of prayer. However, over time, many of us find ourselves in the trenches of leading so it can seem impossible to return to that original place of prayer. Wherever you find yourself in your journey of leadership, I would implore you to carve out space in the war room of prayer like never before.

May we look back at the end of our lives and see a trail of answered prayers following behind us at every stage of the journey. I would encourage you to keep a journal of answered prayers as a way to remind you of all that God is doing in and through your life and leadership.

Remember, *"Nothing of eternal significance happens apart from prayer!"* May we look back and see that lives were transformed because of prayers we dared to pray!

CHAPTER 5

RALLY THE TROOPS

Come Out of the Net!

In a loud, booming, confident tone, the whole team and all the fans heard the words reverberating across the field: "Come out of the net!" That was my dad, who didn't need to be the coach of my soccer team, but was. Talk about an engaged leader! Go Dad!

Let me back up for a moment.

From a very young age, I found a deep passion for the "world's sport," the sport that I think will be played in heaven. (We can dream, right?) Soccer! The OG football!

I was extremely aggressive in the way I played soccer. I never understood anyone who played half-heartedly. I was there to win, and to win decisively.

My passion often caused me to "accidentally" slide tackle a little too often, push shoulders with the opposing team with slightly too much force, and to often have the referees kindly remind me to simmer down.

Then I discovered the most glorious position that exists in the beautiful game.

The keeper or goalie position.

The beautiful part of being a goalie is that you can be as aggressive as you want and tackle as often as you want, as long as you are going for the ball! Now that's what I'm talking about! It was also a micro-manager's paradise because from the keeper's box, you directed the entire team!

Here is what I learned very quickly in my new position: when defending your team, and preventing the opposing team from scoring against you, timing was everything.

There was a time to stay in your box and simply observe everything that went on.

But then, there was that moment when you could not blink or hesitate. This was the moment when you had to punch fear in the face and head right into the heat of the battle. There was that moment when you had to risk it all by leaving the box to face the opposition head on.

Here is where you find my dad screaming out across the field, "Come out of the net, Natalie!" He saw the moment and knew if you don't run all in, you're going to miss the opportunity. If you hesitate, you're toast.

So in these moments of adrenaline surging through my veins, I would come running out of the net, and take the offensive, risking everything for the win.

If only you could hear the voice of my father shouting across this book, "Come out of the net!"

There are crucial moments in leadership when we must no longer simply observe what's happening around us. There are no more variations of strategies that can be written on a whiteboard.

The calculators have to be put away.

There is only one thing we know we must do.

Leave the defensive and jump on the offensive, and with grit in our eyes come running out of the net!

Most of the early stages in the season of innovation as a leader are behind the scenes. It's a time of observation and preparation. But innovation is only truly innovative if it is put into action. How many amazing ideas, solutions, and grand possibilities have gone to the grave with people who were never willing to "come out of the net" and put the vision into play?

There has to come a moment in our leadership when we leave the dreaming stage, we put the post-it notes away, and make our move.

Nehemiah had a crucial "come out of the net" moment in his leadership journey. As we've already seen, he was in a season of preparation and innovation. But then we learn that his heart is stirred to do something. Then, in a behind-the-scenes moment he is praying, asking God how to engage in the needed mission.

It seems rather abrupt and even odd timing when Nehemiah decides to act. It seems that he should have run to the king immediately upon hearing the devastating news of his people. He would have shown more emotion.

Yet he doesn't.

If he isn't running to the king immediately then clearly he is preparing a Ted Talk caliber speech and creating a Google slides presentation to impress. Surely Nehemiah will schedule a summit to lay out the grandiose vision.

Nope. He does neither of these things.

Four months have passed since Nehemiah heard the words that changed everything. It's an ordinary day in the palace. Nehemiah is doing his normal duties. But on this day, he was wearing the weight of the need upon his face.

As Nehemiah is serving the king his wine, the Bible notes he had "never been sad" in the presence of the king. Let's read about it in Nehemiah 2:2-3.

"So the king asked me, "Why are you looking so sad? You don't look sick to me. You must be deeply troubled." *Then I was terrified, but I replied, "Long live the king! How can I not be sad? For the city where my ancestors are buried is in ruins, and the gates have been destroyed by fire."* (NLT)

Here it is. The moment has finally come. Nehemiah is coming out of the net.

On an ordinary day, in the middle of the normal, the burning burden in his heart is about to be broadcasted out.

So the scene plays out like this. The king asks, "Why are you looking so sad?" "You don't look sick. You must be troubled."

In other words. Spill the beans. What's going on with you?

I can almost hear my dad's voice echoing out.

NOW! COME OUT OF THE NET!

This is Nehemiah's moment.

Four months of innovation. Four months of prayer and weeping.

Four months of planning have all led to right here, right now.

Don't miss these crucial words in the narrative.

"Then I was terrified, but I replied."

No one said engaging in a God-sized vision would be without fear.

If the mission you're embarking on doesn't scare you it may not be a God-breathed one.

The moment to finally begin casting the vision, rallying the troops, recruiting a team, comes with more questions than confidence oftentimes.

When it's time to share what's been formulating in your brain, it often comes with the voice of fear screaming in your head.

- "What if it fails?"

- "What if you don't have what it takes?"
- "What if you lose everything in pursuit of this?"
- "What if nobody believes in this with you?"

Engaged leaders hear the same negative narratives. They feel the same fear pulsating through their veins. But something stirs in them that says, "But what if it works?"

Like Nehemiah. "I was terrified… but I replied!"

The greatest risk leaders face is playing it safe. Missing the opportunity to build on your dreams is worse than trying and failing.

Are you scared?

If you answer "Yes," then you're in great company. You're with some of the greatest leaders, innovators, and builders in history.

Lean in. Don't let fear define you.

Here it is, it's your moment to get the word out. It's time to start rallying the troops!

The Elevator Pitch

The button is pressed. The door is closing, meaning the time has arrived, ready or not.

The time has come for the elevator pitch. You've got thirty seconds to throw out a compelling invitation to your "White Hot Why."

I like the way author, Seth Godin, said it on his popular blogging website, *"The purpose of an elevator pitch is to describe a situation or solution so compelling that the person you're with wants to hear more even after the elevator ride is over."*

When you've come out of the net and are ready to speak up, you don't have time to hesitate or formulate a plan. This is when all that you developed and prepared for during the delay is finally about to be put into action.

This is the point at which what's been percolating on the inside of you, gets to be broadcasted to those around you.

When Nehemiah saw his opportunity to speak to the king, he already knew what he wanted to say and was ready to make the big "ask!"

Then the king said to me, *"What are you requesting?"* So I prayed to the God of heaven. And *I said to the king,* "If it pleases the king, and if your servant has found favor in your sight, that you send me to Judah, to the city of my fathers' graves, that I may rebuild it." Nehemiah 2:4–5 (ESV)

Nehemiah goes on to boldly request letters to grant access into the land, as well as for letters to be given the materials needed for the project.

"… And *the king granted me what I asked, for the good hand of my God was upon me."* Nehemiah 2:8b (ESV)

Nehemiah would receive all that he requested because he had rightly prepared in the stage of innovation. Nehemiah knew what his elevator pitch was, and the Lord's favor was upon him.

I truly believe that God favors and opens doors for leaders who seek Him in the place of prayer like Nehemiah, and who are faithful to do their part in the natural place of preparation.

There is always the one-two punch: God's part and our part. Both are necessary. The four months between Nehemiah hearing the need of his people and the city of Jerusalem, and then giving his elevator pitch, were not aimless. He was formulating a compelling pitch to present to the king.

One of the greatest elevator pitches of all time is Jesus inviting His disciples to follow Him: The Passion paraphrase says it like this in Mark 1:16-18:

"As Jesus was walking along the shore of Lake Galilee, he noticed two brothers fishing: Simon and Andrew. He watched them as they were casting their nets into the sea and said to them, "Come follow me and I will transform you into men who catch people instead of fish!" Immediately they dropped their nets and left everything behind to follow Jesus." (TPT)

This documented invitation by Jesus doesn't even last thirty seconds, but the message was so clear that the hearers leave everything behind in order to follow Him.

Jesus gives the pitch, drops the mic, and like an epic movie, doesn't turn around to see the explosion! Simon and Andrew hear it and stop everything they are doing to run after Jesus. They immediately bought the vision Jesus was selling.

This, my friends, is how you begin to rally the troops!

Three Simple Elements Needed for the Initial Vision Casting:

1. **Clarity-** Clarity is your best friend! If you can't say the big idea in one sentence, then you're not ready to give the pitch. Many visions die in the elevator because they were never clearly communicated. Take a play from In-N-Out Burgers playbook. There is no lack of clarity on what they sell! Would you like one patty or two? Jesus' invitation was not vague either. He didn't

use trickery to get what He was asking for. Jesus clearly gave the invitation and kept walking. (We will dive more into clarity in a later chapter.)

Here are three questions to ask yourself as you prepare the pitch:

- o **Is it simple?**- Don't get lost in the details as you try and communicate the vision. Don't over complicate the message, just keep it simple.
- o **Is it consistent?**- There shouldn't be forty variations, or twists, and turns in the pitch. Be consistent in what you say and how you say it.
- o **Is it effective?**- Try your pitch on different people and in different settings. Ask them if the message actually makes sense, does it work, and can they say it back to you.

2. **Compelling-** Give listeners a reason to keep you talking. For example, certain commercials get our attention. We've all had the moment when we are watching a show, and suddenly, a commercial compels us to do something. In the noise of advertising, somebody suddenly cast a message that compels us to action! Jesus' invitation didn't unveil all that following Him would entail, but it compelled them to pursue the one giving

the invitation. The initial vision casting should grip someone to say, "I'm in. Tell me more."

3. **Call to Action-** Tell people what to do next. Jesus' invitation had a clear next step. It demanded movement and action. The call to action was stated in two concise words: "Follow Me!" Your initial invitation must include a clear call to action such as confirmation they are on the team. Nehemiah didn't waste any time giving a call to action to the king. That's one reason why his request was granted.

Remember, this initial communication of the vision is not the time for laying out the whole game plan and providing every strategic step you'll be taking.

This is simply the invite for the interest meeting.

It's the trumpet call to let people know that movement is about to happen. It's to see who definitely wants to be a part of it.

God may give the vision to one man, but He often fulfills it through a team.

Throughout history, one person catches a vision to innovate, to build, reform, and effect change. Their passion, grit, and fire gets them part of the way. But there comes a time when two realities hit them.

"I can't do this alone, nor do I want to do this alone."

Without a leader having innovation and dedication to letting a vision be formed there would be nothing for people to rally behind, but sooner or later the blueprint needs a team to make it leave the paper and become a reality.

Vision may have gotten you this far, but your effectiveness to gather, develop, and deploy a team will determine how far you will actually go!

It takes a leader to begin to see what no one else can see. But it takes a team to build what that leader sees!

One of my husband's and my favorite places to visit is Disneyland. Need I say more?

It truly is a magical place and brings wonder to children and adults alike.

There are an estimated eighteen million visitors a year to Disneyland and fifty-three million visitors a year to Disney World. Most of us couldn't imagine a world without Disneyland and those churros, am I right?

This vision all started in the heart and mind of one man, Walt Disney. After twenty years Mr. Disney saw the dream of this magical place come alive when the gates opened on July 17th, 1955. This incredible visionary and dreamer saw a beautiful place that no one else saw. This dream may have been birthed in the heart of one man, yet it took some two thousand, five hundred workers to build the initial park, and make the dream come alive!

A leader saw what no one else could see, but he accomplished the dream through a team who gave of themselves in order to see it become a reality.

Over the next few chapters, we will begin looking at how we as leaders transition from the stage of innovation and move to the stage of motivation.

Leader, you have something that needs to be built. There is a mission worth pursuing. Now, may we give of ourselves to rallying the troops and motivating our teams to engage in this beautiful cause!

- MOTIVATE-

| mo·ti·vate |

Phase 2

Motive 1: something (such as a need or desire) that causes a person to act.

Motivate: to provide with a motive.

The Motivate phase of engaged leadership is often the stage that most leaders are tempted to skip, yet it is the linchpin stage for lasting success in building and reaching the desired leadership outcome.

This phase of leadership is all about getting clarity around the mission and vision, and then making the big ask before you begin to activate the team!

This is the moment where your personal leadership innovation begins to be communicated to the team around you. It's where your vision becomes their vision, your passion becomes their passion, and what captivated you now begins to captivate them.

How long should you take in this phase?

As long as it takes!

The motivation stage will often feel long and tedious for the leader, but it's the vital moment of engaging your team to the vision, so they can then become activated in the vision. The danger we often face in leadership is seeing the gifts in individuals and deploying them before they have been mobilized and bought into the mission and vision.

I liken the phase of motivation as being like the final checks before a rocket ship is to be launched. The destination (space) is clearly defined prior to launch, yet there are great precautions taken prior to launch to make sure everything is in perfect working order. There are zero apologies made when a mission is temporarily aborted due to some form of malfunction. **The team knows that delay of the mission is far greater than the death of a mission.**

Recently a planned launch of the "SpaceX Falcon Rocket" was aborted one second prior to takeoff. One second! A member of the launch team announced engine start and liftoff. A second later, she said, "Disregard. We have an abort."

This is a great example for us to follow as engaged leaders. Our objective is to effectively get the team to the final destination in one piece and on mission. The time, energy, and attention we give in the season of motivation will determine our effectiveness in the place of activation!

Remember: Motivation must always precede Activation!

CHAPTER 6

SIGN ON THE DOTTED LINE!

Why Didn't You Just Tell Me?

I may be biased, but I am married to the most incredible man. To know Riley is to be blessed. Why do I start this chapter here? The following story requires you to know that contrary to its content, he really is amazing! Moving on.

For our honeymoon, Riley planned an amazing vacation to the beautiful island of Kauai. This was my first time on any of the Hawaiian islands, and I got bit with the bug! Take me back!

If you've ever been to Hawaii you know the glorious wonder of "Hawaiian Shave Ice." Don't you dare say, "Isn't that just a snow cone?" If you uttered those words, then you have clearly not had true "Hawaiian shave ice."

This stuff is magical. Refreshing. If your taste buds could hug you after eating it, they would.

There was a hip, shaved ice food truck near our resort. We found it on the first full day we were there and let's just say we found our way back to it a fair share more times.

I remember day after day we would go to order and Riley would say, "Do you want to share one?" In my head I was thinking, "Share one, are you kidding me? Honey, give me the biggest size they have!"

As his new beloved, sweet bride, I would smile and say, "Share? Absolutely! My pleasure!"

So each day we would wait in line and go through the same thing, sharing the shaved ice, although I longingly desired more!

I finally mustered up the courage on the last day we were there.

This was my moment.

I was going to swing for the fence and ask for my own shaved ice. We were driving around the island, and were going to be flying out in a few short hours.

Here in our small SUV, I made the big ask… "Hey babe, maybe today when we, ummm, get some, ah, shaved ice… Uh, can I get my own?"

My dear husband immediately responded, "Absolutely, have you wanted your own the whole time? Why didn't you just tell me?"

In his defense, I always want to share. I typically end up giving Riley half of my food anyways, that is until I had Hawaiian Shave Ice!

For the record, Riley now always offers to buy me my own shaved ice! He would have been delighted to not share with me in Hawaii as well but I simply never asked.

The teams we lead are made up of individuals who are desperate for us to simply and clearly state what it is we are asking. They are crying out for us to "just tell them" what it is we want from them.

People are desperate to follow a grand vision. They want to give their lives to building something that matters. Yet, oftentimes, we fail to rally people to the cause because we don't clarify what it is that we are asking them to join.

There is endless potential bound up in the lives of people around us, but it will remain untouched until a leader comes along and clearly lays out the invitation to join them in building.

If there is a stage in our leadership journey we are often tempted to skip, it's this stage of motivating the team around a clearly defined mission.

The temptation of a leader who has their "White Hot Why" moment and has now courageously come out of the net to invite others to join, is to start running towards the goal, not paying attention to the fact that no one knows where or why they are running!

Now that you've got their attention, it's time to tell them why you have it!

The stage of motivation is to lay out the "Big Picture" of what you're inviting them to join without hesitation or impatience.

Helpful Steps in Clarifying the Vision to the Team:

- **Be up front-** I love when I see the words, "NO HIDDEN FEES!" There is nothing more frustrating when getting ready to hit the purchase button and at the last minute you're tricked with additional "servicing fees." When we cast the vision we must be up front and clear about what it is we are doing and the part we see them playing. This is where clarity is essential. There should be no question in which direction you are heading and the desired final destination. Like a flight attendant giving the final call of where this plane is going, we must communicate where this mission is directed. Before that plane ever takes off, every passenger is aware of what they signed up for!

- **Ask Big-** Oftentimes our danger as leaders is not setting the bar too high for people, but rather never making the big ask and giving people the opportunity to rise to the occasion. In the stage of motivation and rallying the team around the vision, we must ask for big commitment and all-in dedication. The team you want around you is a team that doesn't run from the big ask or commitment but is spurred onward to make it happen. We see in the culture around us that people will leave better paying jobs in order to give more time and energy to the company that has a grander vision! You can make bold requests of your team if you have a big vision. Not only do our teams need us to be up front about where we are going, they also need us to be bold and clear about what level of commitment we are asking them to make. Remember it is easier to ask big than to ask for a little bit and then keep coming back to ask for more. Before you engage in the conversation with your team about what you are asking them to do, write it down and make sure you understand what it is you are asking them to commit to. We often fail to ask big because we have failed to plan and are unaware of what we need them to commit to. Never underestimate the hunger in your team. They are often waiting for the opportunity to rise to the occasion if we would simply ask big of them!

- **Listen Closely-** If you want to know how clearly you're communicating vision, listen to your team as they communicate back what they just heard. I have finished sharing at many meetings with my teams, and thought to myself, "Wow, I nailed it," only to have myself brought back to reality when a team member shared and I realize they did not catch what I was trying to communicate. We must create intentional space to hear back from our teams what they are hearing us say. If they can't clearly communicate the vision back to us, we are not ready to move forward. Note: this can be painfully frustrating as a leader because we often have to communicate the vision over and over again until we hear in the language of our team that they have caught it! John Maxwell wisely said it like this, *"The first time you say something, it's heard. The second time, it's recognized, and the third time it's learned."* If our team can't repeat the vision back to us, we must keep working out ways to clearly communicate the vision. If we listen closely we will either hear the sound of a team on mission together or a team in confusion.

Are You With Me?

Clearly laying out the vision as a leader doesn't mean everyone will want to join you in building it, and that is very good news!

Our job as leaders is to clarify where we are going and what we want people to do in order to make it happen. However, their job is to make a decision as to whether they will commit to that vision.

In other words, *our job is to clarify what we are asking, but theirs is to commit to it.*

Even the best laid out plans led by a once-in-a-generation leader will still have people deciding not to sign up for the mission. This doesn't mean you're a bad leader. It often means you've done an excellent job communicating the vision and they understand the commitment required, and now they can make a conscious decision to commit or walk away.

Knowing who is not with you is often just as important as knowing who is with you.

Before you head into the season of activation and building, you need to know who it is that is ready to commit to the vision so you can begin building.

We must remember that clarity goes both ways. As leaders, it is our job to make the expectations explicitly clear, but it is also our job to require clarification from the team as to where they are at.

Practical Tips on Identifying Who is With You:

- **Make sure they are claiming to be on the team**- As leaders we often see someone and think, "They would be perfect to lead this part of the team." We can already have their whole next twelve months mapped out before they have committed to the team. You must hear from their own mouth, "This is my team, my mission, my tribe, my wall to build, etc." Before you can claim them as your own, they must claim you as their own! Listen to the language as they communicate with you. It's a red flag when everything they are saying is impersonal and calling the team "your team" and not "their team." Someone who is committed to being on the team begins to communicate in a language that expresses their personal interest and investment.

- **Don't beg for them to stay-** If someone has not bought in when you've cast the vision and clarified the mission, you may need to just move on. If you have to convince them to join the team in the beginning, you'll have to beg them to stay when the going gets tough. This can be initially painful when people you were convinced would be building alongside you choose to go another way. But this can also be one of the greatest gifts given to you when building a team for the long haul. When someone is with you, you don't have to chase them down or persuade them to join. Instead, they take the initiative to run alongside you.

- **Celebrate who is with you!-** There is a snare that every leader can fall into, and that's to grieve about who is not with you instead of celebrating who is. People need to see us as leaders rejoicing and believing in the ones who are with us, not weeping over those who didn't join the team or who leave the team. We build with who is with us, not those we hoped would be with us! As the old adage goes, "Don't judge a book by its cover." Likewise, don't be surprised by the ones who end up coming alongside you. Often it isn't who we expected, but it turns out better than we could have ever imagined!

- **Get names on the roster before positions on the field-** Avoid the snare of trying to recruit people by promising them a specific position. Before you begin identifying "what" they will do, make sure you know "who" is with you. It's crucial that someone is committed to the vision and not just a position. We must be careful not to build a role around a specific person, but rather have a role that is clearly defined for a team member to step in and fill. After the team is identified, then you can begin to get them mobilized and poised for action!

Nehemiah was well aware of the team that was with him as well as those who chose to not be builders on the wall. Chapter 3 lists name after name of people and families that were building the wall. Yet verse five notes one group of nobles that would not "stoop to serve." "And next to them the Tekoites repaired, but *their nobles would not stoop to serve their Lord.*" Nehemiah 3:5 ESV

Nehemiah modeled the crucial leadership tool of "knowing his team." He was not naive to the ones who were committed to the cause and those that he would be unable to depend upon. We don't get insight as to how or when Nehemiah became aware of this, but we know that at some point in the season of vision casting, there were those who arose to build and those who backed away.

Let's Do This

Timing is an essential tool in the belt of a leader. The right timing of when to move forward doesn't always follow a specific time frame or process. You can have a game plan and targeted date for the team to be ready, but oftentimes the readiness of the team doesn't line up exactly with that.

All throughout the Bible and history we see that great leaders develop a sense of timing. They are aware of when their team is ready to engage in the battle, and when they need to put the breaks on and intentionally develop the team further.

Nehemiah was exemplary in understanding the timing of leadership. He was sensitive to the timing of when he would ask the king to be released. He was calculated as to when he finally cast the vision to the people about building the wall. He engaged rapidly when he saw the readiness of his team to build.

There comes a point in the stage of motivation that you can see the readiness of the team to begin to activate and step out. Something shifts in their language, eyes, and behavior. There is a shift from observation to hunger for participation. A cry begins to rise up out of them, "LET'S DO THIS!"

There is a critical moment when that happened in the stage of motivation in Nehemiah's leadership. Nehemiah simply cast a clear and compelling vision, and the people cried out to take action. After months of preparation, journeying, and inspecting the land, Nehemiah knew that now was the time to invite the people to fully engage in the mission.

"Then I said to them, "You see the trouble we are in, how Jerusalem lies in ruins with its gates burned. Come, let us build the wall of Jerusalem, that we may no longer suffer derision." And I told them of the hand of my God that had been upon me for good, and also of the words that the king had spoken to me. And they said, "Let us rise up and build." So they strengthened their hands for the good work."
Nehemiah 2:18-19. ESV

What an incredible scene and example of getting buy-in from the team prior to activating them. Nehemiah shares the need, tells the story of what God has already done, and the people are begging to start building.

- **Cast a vision worth dying for-** People want to give their life for something that matters, something that will live beyond their years, something worth dying for. Nehemiah did not sugar coat the mission and need. He painted the full picture and the people were stirred. We must lay before our teams a vision that's worth going all in for, something worth giving everything to see it come to fruition. We must never allow fear or anything else to keep us from casting a vision that is worth dying for!

- **Simply tell the story-** This is the time to tell people about the journey and tell the story of how you came upon this mission and burden. Bring people on the journey with you, where they can begin to see their place inside of the story that God is writing. They may not have been there when you received the burning vision, but invite them in so they can begin to catch their own passion in the middle of the narrative. Don't just cast the vision, invite people into the story of the vision, and share with them how God has already been working.

- **Wait for the passion to emerge-** Those who are going to engage the mission wholeheartedly will hear the vision and very rapidly will begin to have their own passion emerge. It suddenly goes from being your thing, to our thing. There is a hunger that emerges, and your team is no longer talking about the problem, but becoming part of the SOLUTION! Watch closely. When you see the passion emerge, you'll know you are on the brink of activation in accomplishing the mission!

How will you know that your team is ready to begin to prepare for activation? They begin to cry out, "Let us rise up and build." There begins to be a desperation to get in the trenches and to get dirty. Your team will be eager to make that which has only been a dream, become a reality!

CHAPTER 7
HELP THEM FIND THEIR PLACE!

I got this brilliant spark of genius and inspiration around the age of twenty-two. I realized I needed to learn a new skill, find an outlet to express myself, and relax. I needed a hobby!

Then it struck me... The hobby I needed to take up was art -- painting to be more specific. I reached out to my friend who is a professional artist. People actually pay for her incredible work!

I shared my newfound desire to take up a relaxing hobby and thus learn art with her.

So we set a time to get together and start the training. Part one of our first evening together was going to the store and buying all of the gear. After all, real artists need good equipment. After getting the necessary tools to launch into my newfound passion (at least my pre-passion, I hadn't actually done anything artsy yet!), we headed back to base camp to embark on creating the next Mona Lisa or something Michelangelo would be inspired by.

For the next hour or so my friend began to set up our station. She passionately explained the purpose of each tool and gave some details about our first project. Finally, after a few hours, it was time to begin my new pursuit of art!

Here is the part of the story where we discover this was a terrible idea.
Seriously, a terrible one.

It took a matter of minutes to discover there is not an ounce of a painter in me. My art looked like a two-year-old attacked the paint and smeared it all over the canvas. It was hard to tell if I used guacamole or paint.

If you don't believe me, I have proof. My painting got left out at my parent's house and a sweet lady asked my mom, "Oh wow, did a little kid give you that?"

"Umm, no my young adult daughter made it!"

By the way, my own mother didn't even keep my art. Thanks, Mom.

Not only did I discover in my first moments of art that I was terrible, but I also realized that I could care less about this hobby. You couldn't pay me enough to want to try and develop this talent. I realized this was not my gift mix and I needed to let the artists be artists. And I would not ever be part of that group!

As I came to the reality that it was time to try a new hobby, I saw a master at work as my friend took these simple art tools and created something of beauty and excellence.

She was in her element, her gifts were shining, and you could see her using gifts that God had placed upon her life. She knew her place and confidently walked in it.

In the same moment, it became obvious that one person needed to never touch a paintbrush again, and the other would be robbing the world if they didn't use the gift of God.

I have never attempted painting again. The world is better for it, trust me. My friend has used her gift of art as she lived on the mission field helping illiterate people with illustrations that taught them proper hygiene that could save their lives. She also recently started an art company for teaching children and teens art! She has truly engaged in her God-given gifting and the world is better for it!

As engaged leaders, it is essential that we personally are self-aware of not only our strengths but especially our weaknesses. It is equally important that we are creating a healthy culture around us that helps people identify their place and gifting, and then confidently walk in them. Our job is not to simply throw people out into the mission and tell them to figure it out, our job is to position them for the win!

When people are engaged in the right place on the team, it not only is a win for them personally but it is a win for the overall team and mission.

In the motivation stage, we must identify the abilities and skills of those who are going to be on our team. Like a builder who assesses the tools and materials they have to work with, we must assess the building potential that is in the people gathered around us.

Now that we know:

- ○ What we are building and who is with us to build it.
- ○ We can now begin to identify where each person will build!

In the Initial Stages of Identifying the Best Placement of Each Team Member, There are a Few Things to Look For:

- **Look for the passion-** Like a fire, passion simply needs a little fuel for it to be unrelenting. When you cast the vision and identify a team member for a specific task or position, you should begin to see the passion rise as they consider how they will meet the need. Oftentimes you can quickly identify someone's skill set by asking them this question: "What is the number one thing we need to fix or give our focus to?" The first thing they identify as the most important is often the source of their passion, which indicates where they should be placed. When a leader is passionate about a specific area, they will often be willing to help serve there, even if they don't have a title or compensation for it. Their passion drives them to want to be engaged no matter what.

- **Look for pursuit-** When someone has the gift potential for a specific area they pursue it with hunger and desire to develop that area. You won't have to beg them to develop something. They will instinctively look for mentors, resources, and tools to help them succeed in that specific area. They will pursue innovative ideas, identify like-minded people to build with, and do anything and everything that would cause them to be at peak effectiveness in this area. When you see their personal pursuit increase, it's a clear sign that they are doing what they should be doing.

- **Look for productivity-** The fruit doesn't lie! An apple tree produces apples, and someone that is in their sweet spot of gifting will begin to bear delicious fruit in their assigned area. There will be signs even in the early stages that they are effective in this specific role and skill. People can get it in their heads that they have a particular skill set, but they have to prove it with their actions and their fruit. So look for the evidence related to production and effectiveness, which confirms they have the right gift mix. Someone with the potential to be a strong team leader will have people rallying around them. They will be successfully communicating at the grassroots level, and later on a larger scale. As you see them advancing in their skills, increasing their influence, being fruitful and productive, you will know that you did a good job of positioning that person on the team.

Finding Their 10

Pastor Chris Hodges says this, *"Everybody is a 10 somewhere!"*

The question is not, "Does each person have potential or a specific skill set inside of them?" The question is, "Am I willing to engage in the work of helping each person discover their 10?"

The job of an engaged leader is to not only innovate and cast vision, but it is to also motivate and develop people so they can be activated in the vision. The job of a leader looks much like the job of a miner. We go into the dirty and deep recesses of the mine to harvest the treasure we know lies within.

Our job is to create a healthy environment where people can discover, develop, and deploy their gifts. We must create a culture where people can truly find their 10!

- **Discover**- People don't always recognize their gifts or they tend to undervalue them. Some fail to realize that their gift is special, and many think that everybody is able to do what they do so well. Therefore, a good leader is trained to see the glimmer of gifting inside an individual before they personally recognize it. It's amazing how a leader's recognition of a person plants the seed of potential and fuels faith for the future. Many people throughout history spoke of a coach, teacher, pastor, or leader in their life who saw something special in them and encouraged them to succeed! As engaged leaders, we must create intentional pathways for people to identify potential so they can effectively develop those gifts.

- **Develop-** One of the greatest gifts we can instill in the team around us is an insatiable hunger to develop their gifts and abilities. Potential means very little if it never gets developed and put into action. We can help shine a light on someone's potential but it's up to the individual to pursue the development of that gift. One example is the preparation process for a TED Talk. These speakers spend months and months in personal preparation, some spending fifteen to twenty hours with a TED talk coach to improve their speech. Some speakers give one hundred hours of their personal time for speech development and preparation. Obviously, these speakers are committed to developing their gift to achieve peak performance. They are diving into developing that gift to max capacity. Good leaders are aware of how important it is to create a culture that fosters growth and development, as well as celebrates the individual who fully engages in this process.

- **Deploy-** We must create opportunities for people to deploy their gifts and abilities. Part of the development process requires putting the gift into action. As you see gifts being honed and developed, use your wisdom to create opportunities for that individual to use them. If we are going to have a healthy culture, we have to give people the opportunity to succeed or even to fail. It takes real "at-bats" to learn how to connect with the ball. Most advanced college degrees combine the study of books for head knowledge with hands-on experience in a safe environment. This is how people learn how to put their knowledge and gift into action. Therefore, we must create hands-on opportunities for people to begin to deploy their gifting.

Coach with a Leadership Pipeline!

Creating a healthy team culture needs to look a lot more like coaching college athletics than professional sports. A college coach knows that no matter how skilled their player is, he only has four years max to develop their skills. Oftentimes, the player may not be of any help to the coach or team until their senior year. But the coach knows they have to keep a pipeline flowing on their team where they are constantly discovering, developing, and deploying athletes. The minute that coach stops any one of these three stages, they are toast.

As leaders, we must assess if we truly have a strong leadership pipeline. We must be engaged with the team on the field, but always engaged in discovering, developing, and deploying new team members. Like a college coach, we must be intentional, making the best use of the time we have with each individual that is on our team while creating consistent pathways for new team members to come on board.

Grab Your Brick

When Nehemiah began to cast the vision and rally the troops to join him in this grand mission, it was with an usual group of people that would not normally be placed together. His team consisted of nobles and ordinary people alike. It was a grouping of young and old building side by side. From the outside looking in, it may have seemed like a strange mix of people, but they were united by a common vision and each knew their place in the mission.

How did this happen?

By serving under a strategic leader who knew the importance of positioning each individual in the best place possible. Nehemiah knew what it was going to take to not only build the wall but to continue to protect it. That's why he was committed to building the best team to accomplish all phases of his project.

How do you build and restore two-and-a-half miles of a wall in a mere fifty-two days? First, by having the grace and power of God with you. But also through a united group of people, each knowing their individual place on the wall and each committed to building where they were. As you read through the book of Nehemiah, you see there was clarity around the vision and clarity in relation to assignments.

Immediately after the wall is built, Nehemiah begins to strategically put people in their place of effectiveness to continue moving the city forward.

"Now when the wall had been built and I had set up the doors, and the gatekeepers, the singers, and the Levites had been appointed, I gave my brother Hanani and Hananiah the governor of the castle charge over Jerusalem, for he was a more faithful and God-fearing man than many. …. Appoint guards from among the inhabitants of Jerusalem, some at their guard posts and some in front of their own homes." Nehemiah 7:1–2, 3b (ESV)

Nehemiah begins placing gatekeepers, singers, Levites, city leaders, and guards from among the people. This happened quickly because Nehemiah was paying attention to his people. He knew who would be the right fit for each position to effectively accomplish the second phase of his vision.

When you have people in the right place on the team, there is no stopping the effectiveness of that team. People who are committed to the task at hand, who know their place and who are equipped with the tools to make it happen, are the people you are ready to activate! There is nothing worse than beginning to build with the wrong team. John Maxwell sums it up very well. "Teamwork makes the dream work, but a vision becomes a nightmare when the leader has a big dream and a bad team."

It is worth the extra time to clarify who is with you and where they need to be. When you put the work in at the stage of motivation, it leads to future success in the stage of activation. The outside world may wonder "What's taking so long? Why haven't they started yet?" But when you've laid the foundation correctly and honed in on the right team, it will look like you were an overnight success.

You will not regret the time you spend laying out the vision, rallying the troops, and getting people in their best position. There is nothing quite like seeing the faces of team members who believe in the vision and are willing to bring their individual bricks to build something far bigger than themselves.

How do you build a cathedral? Brick by brick. How do you begin to build the vision that God has asked you to engage with? By activating a team in which each person brings their bricks and together build something beautiful!

CHAPTER 8
TWO WINGS OF CULTURE

Culture Matters

I love Chick-fil-A!

Yep. Give me one of their ice-cold lemonades, chicken strips, waffle fries, and lots of sauce! If you haven't tried their Honey Roasted BBQ Sauce, do it! You'll thank me later. My husband and I love it so much that we map out many of our road trips around being able to hit up a Chick-fil-A! Just a few months ago, the very first Chick-fil-A opened in our city about five minutes from our house. (Hence the reason I needed to write this book. Thanks for contributing to our waffle fries fund!)

Actually, more than I like their food, I love their culture. I'm fascinated by the culture of hospitality and service that you find in every one of their restaurants all across the country. I intentionally say thank you as many times as possible just to test if the employee will carry on the culture of replying with, "My pleasure!"

In case you're wondering, they are doing a great job carrying on that culture piece! Oftentimes an employee will come to your table and ask if you need anything and then ask, "Can I refresh your beverage?" Even the language of refresh versus refill sounds hospitable!

Chick-fil-A has something in their culture they call their "Core 4" that their employees are to do in their interactions with guests.

- Make Eye Contact
- Smile
- Speak Enthusiastically
- Stay Connected (or make a connection)

These four simple things are just one way Chick-fil-A staff embody their value and culture of "Customer First."

There is nothing like seeing an organization or team of people who embrace their culture in such a way that you can identify their values before you ever see them framed on the wall.

One thing that engaged leaders understand is that culture matters. It really, really matters.

When a leader and their organization have a healthy culture it changes everything, but when a culture is unhealthy, it is not a pretty thing. We've all walked into a room where the culture is off and the team isn't in unity. You want to run away as fast as possible! The word "awkward" comes to mind!

Cultivating a healthy culture takes intentionality and hard work, but it's worth every minute that goes into it. A vibrant healthy culture is often the very thing that differentiates the good from the great.

You can have a vision and "White Hot Why" that's worth dying for, but you must create a healthy environment for that vision to thrive in.

Start Right

As I mentioned earlier, we recently had a Chick-fil-a open in our town. A few years before that, we had the first In-N-Out Burger in Oregon open in our city. Yes, I know that we are highly favored!

There was something really intriguing that both companies did before they opened. For the first few weeks before the businesses were launched, both companies brought in "Culture Carriers." These were trained staff from all over the country who arrived to set the culture and tone of the restaurant as it opened. These trained employees led the way alongside the new local hires. They were modeling the culture and atmosphere they wanted right from the start.

Most companies would say, "Hey, we just opened, people will give us a break if it's not all hammered out right away." But these organizations knew that the way they started would largely impact how they continued. They knew the importance and power of creating the right habits and culture from opening day.

Is it possible to fix an unhealthy culture in your team or organization?

Yes.

But it's a lot more effective to identify and establish your culture before you start building.

In the final stage of "motivation," it's crucial that your team is aware of the culture you are attempting to establish and that they become the greatest champions of this culture.

Culture building is something you must cultivate both in the season of motivation and activation. You can't just "Set it and forget it." Culture is constantly being challenged and must be continually re-evaluated, assessed, adjusted, and cultivated.

Culture building done in the stage of motivation will greatly enhance the fruit you see as you activate the team to build.

Engage in Building a Healthy Culture

- **Create the Culture-** You cannot delegate the creation of your team's culture to someone else. If the culture is not deeply personal and something you believe in, you will not pay the price to cultivate it. It's vital that you know the atmosphere and distinctives that will mark what you are building. What is it that you want to be marked by? What is the thing you hope fifty years from now people will say, "He gave everything to live out that value"? As you create the culture you want, it must be more than words on a plaque, but rather the hill you're willing to die on!

- **Champion the Culture-** People follow the behaviors of a leader, not just the values they read in their handbooks. You are the number one champion of the culture that you want to build. People will follow your behaviors and practices. The best way to teach the culture you are creating is to model the culture to the team around you! Your team is watching you and waiting to follow what you model! They become your champions.

- **Communicate the Culture-** What matters to you is what you will communicate on a consistent basis. Vision and culture leak. If you aren't talking about it, your team definitely isn't talking about it. Like John Maxwell said, *"The first time you say something, it's heard. The second time, it's recognized, and the third time it's learned."* You must create an environment where the culture you want is constantly being communicated. People need to be able to repeat back to you your culture, and be able to communicate the clear pathways to achieve that culture. Keep talking, continue sharing the vision, and when you think it's too much, say it again!

- **Celebrate the Culture-** What you celebrate will be repeated. This can work in your favor towards the building of a healthy culture, or it can reveal that the culture doesn't really matter. We must be careful and aware of what it is we are celebrating and highlighting in our teams. Are we rewarding behavior that undermines the culture we want, or are we celebrating the behind-the-scenes demonstrations of the culture we are building? Be generous with celebrating the right things. Compliment and highlight the team because they are carrying the heart of the culture you have envisioned.

- **Check the Culture-** Feedback is your best friend! Culture must constantly be evaluated and assessed. There needs to be clear feedback loops that let you know if you are living out the culture you want built. One rule of thumb for evaluating culture is to assess something as often as it happens. If you are running something weekly, then have a weekly feedback loop. If it's a yearly event, then it needs a yearly evaluation. The team needs to see that you will continually be assessing the cultural wins and making adjustments accordingly! (We will talk more about this later in the book.)

- **Correct the Culture-** If it's broken, fix it! Culture doesn't really mean anything if we are unwilling to enforce it and use the necessary tools to fix it. Recently, I was in a meeting with some of my team and I violated culture by something I said. Immediately someone on my team respectively called me out for my violation of culture. My response? I stopped and apologized to all that were present for my culture-breaking moment, and I corrected my wrong response (while also eating some humble pie). My team did exactly what I would want them to do; they upheld culture and were even willing to call me out when I was tearing it down! If you aren't willing to correct negative culture, it doesn't matter enough to you, and your team will immediately know that! Patrick Lencioni says it well, "*A core value is something you're willing to get punished for.*" You know that you've established a cultural value if you're willing to pay the price for violating it.

Give Them the Keys

Within days of turning 16, I was at the DMV taking my driving test. I did it. I passed the test and got the awkward picture you get to keep for years. The real defining moment though was when I got home after I had a freshly minted license. That was when my parents handed me the keys to my 1997 Saturn and let me go for my first spin without them!

Side note: For some reason, the first place I decided to drive was to the library and donut shop. What a magical first expedition out!

Having a driver's license allowed me to legally drive, but my parents handing me the keys was the empowerment I needed to use this newfound authority.

As we begin to motivate the team and prepare them for activation, we must also empower them. We must hand them the keys, and give them permission to mobilize for movement. The greatest army for building and strengthening the culture you want to build is by empowering the team around you.

As the leader, you must create the culture you desire but not become the bottleneck for that culture. Now is the time to empower the team around you to begin to build and protect cultural norms and values. If you want to build effectively you've got to hand them the keys and let them take a few spins!

Tools and Weapons: The Two Wings of Culture-

We come to a few pivotal moments in the leadership of Nehemiah and the empowering of his team.

We know that he cast the vision to build the wall and that the people are chomping at the bit to be a part of the process. We know that Nehemiah then strategically places people in the right place to build. He then empowers the people to build by placing the right tools and materials in their hands. All throughout chapter three of Nehemiah, we learn about people laying beams, setting doors, repairing the walls, and more. Nehemiah hands the proverbial keys to the people and empowers them to build and to begin the work that was in front of them.

As the people began to build, there was an immediate verbal attack thrust at the people and aimed to stop the building.

Even the best plans and strategies will have opposition and threats that come against them. Engaged leaders don't buckle under such an attack, but with wisdom, they empower their teams to build despite it and to remain focused.

In the face of opposition, Nehemiah doesn't shield his people, he EMPOWERS them!

The greatest advocates for your mission and culture are not outsiders, they are the team that is on the wall building. If you want to know who are the real threats and enemies of your culture, ask your team members, the ones who are busy building. They can tell you exactly what is happening within your organization.

Nehemiah hears the threats, sees the enemy, and thus empowers his team to use their tools and weapons. " ... *Those who carried burdens were loaded in such a way that each labored on the work with one hand and held his weapon with the other. And each of the builders had his sword strapped at his side while he built...*" **Nehemiah 4:17b–18a (ESV)**

Nehemiah hands his team the two wings of culture.

Tools to Build and Weapons to Tear Down

Nehemiah empowers his team to build what matters and to war against anything coming to stop the mission.

As Leaders We Must Empower Teams With Two Elements:

Tools to build

Our teams need to be empowered with the necessary resources, training, and authority to build a healthy culture. Much of our job is equipping our teams with everything they need to get the job done and eliminate any bottlenecks to progress.

Weapons to tear down

Those on the front lines of building are the best voices to make us aware of the potential enemies and snares that are in the trenches of building. We must equip the team with the proper weapons to combat culture busters. They must be empowered to stop the threat right where it is. As they are building a healthy culture in your organization, they need the authority and resources to stop the spread of an unhealthy habit or philosophy that is contrary to the culture.

Own It

What do I see when a group of people have dirt on their face, swords by their sides, and tools in their hands? I see a group of people who bought into a vision and are ready to build something that is bigger than just one person's vision.

I see a group of people who are invested, taking ownership, engaged, and ready to make something happen!

When you hear the language switch from "This is your thing," to "This is *our* thing," you have a team that is motivated, equipped, and ready to build! This is a team that is ready to take action and make something happen.

The late Jack Welch, one of the greatest CEOs of all time, said this "No company, small or large, can win over the long run without energized employees who believe in the mission and understand how to achieve it."

When people believe in the mission and they can see their place in the big picture, there are no limits to what they will do to make it happen. These are the people who are willing to risk everything to protect the culture of the team and to ensure that what needs to be done gets accomplished!

As leaders, it's crucial to know what we are building. However, it's equally important that we take the time to build the culture we want on our team as we build it.

Now that we know where we are going, and how we are getting there, it's time to activate our teams and start building!

- ACTIVATE-

| ac·ti·vate |

Phase 3

Active 1: characterized by action rather than by contemplation or speculation

an active life 2: producing or involving action or movement.

Activate: to make active or more active: to become active.

The final phase of activation is where the boots hit the ground, and the team is activated to build what has been set before them! This phase requires intentional involvement with the team and the culture that you are building.

This is when the blueprint begins to turn into a tangible structure and reality. It's when the team leaves the huddle of motivation and begins to activate the play on the field.

Though it's the final phase of the deployment of vision, it is really just the launching zone for you as the leader and for the team around you.

CHAPTER 9
PLAYING FOR THE NAME ON THE FRONT OF THE JERSEY

The Star Spangled Banner and Teamwork-

Every four years my patriotism and love of all things red white and blue skyrockets. "Why?" you might ask. The Olympics, of course!

I absolutely love the Olympics! Suddenly I become very interested in sports I didn't even know existed. I don't think my husband entirely gets my extreme passion to stay up into the wee hours of the night to cheer on our curling team or the power walkers! (If you want a good laugh, just look up some of the oddest Olympic sports from the past.)

I love cheering on American athletes who have given their lives to mastering their sport and are representing our nation in their area of expertise. There is something so uniting when you hear national anthems play from each winning nation, and you see the athletes representing their people with pride and joy.

It's amazing to me that every one of these athletes who have devoted themselves personally, then unite together to play for the success of their team --
more than for their own personal success.

The Olympics are one of the greatest examples of where the name on the front of the jersey matters more than the personal name on the back.

Each athlete is rooting for their fellow Olympians because when they win, the whole team wins!

Suddenly, basketball players who were former competitors in the NBA, are now teammates cheering each other on. It's a time when each athlete is totally invested in the success of the overall team, not just their personal success.

A healthy team culture is one in which each individual is invested in the success of the team more than their personal success. As we activate our teams, we want to activate a team culture that is one heart, one vision, and one mind: A culture where each individual personally develops their personal skills and abilities in order to better the overall success of the whole team! A culture where the name on the front of the jersey matters more than their name on the back.

The gravitational pull that hits individuals on a team is the temptation to play for their own success or personal gain. No matter how many cute sayings and mantras your organization has about the power of teamwork, if a culture of true teamwork is not cultivated, it will not happen on its own. It takes intentional leadership to activate a culture where each individual lays aside their personal agendas and gifts and agrees to do whatever it takes to build what's best for everybody else.

If this sounds counter-culture, you're right.

Much of what we are fed in schools of leadership, universities, and through observing the world around us, is a dog-eat-dog culture. You better climb the corporate ladder fast and if you crunch some fingers of people you pass by, it's just par for the course.

We've all observed the sports teams that had massive budgets and tried to "buy a championship" with multi-million-dollar contracts. But money can't fabricate a united team. Selfless teamwork is a choice and is cultivated through a lot of intentional hard work.

Even those who walked closest to Jesus struggled with grasping a new paradigm of leadership called Servant Leadership.

The disciples were wondering who got to ride shotgun next to Jesus and who was the greatest. This didn't really sit well with the rest of the team. I don't think it was because they were noble. More likely they were wondering why they didn't think about asking first!

The view of leadership was skewed in Jesus' disciples, much like it is in our culture today. The following Scripture reveals the masterful, flipping our worldview of leadership on its head philosophy of Jesus.

"So Jesus called them together and said, "You know that the rulers in this world lord it over their people, and officials flaunt their authority over those under them. But among you it will be different. Whoever wants to be a leader among you must be your servant," **Mark 10:42–43 (NLT)**

"But among you it will be different." I love these words of Jesus.

I am provoked in my personal leadership to walk these Scriptures out. Jesus has given this call to action to lead and build teams differently.

Jesus knew His mission. He knew what He was building.

Jesus knew how he would build it. He was not intimidated or shaped by the culture around Him, but rather He shaped the culture around Him.

This is what engaged leaders do!

Jesus acknowledged that there was a way that the world leads, but then He laid out a different plan of leadership that His followers would grab hold of.

It is Important That As You Build With Your Team and Shape the Team Culture, You Do a Few Things:

- **Acknowledge**- As leaders, we must acknowledge there are different ways to build and that other teams will adopt different strategies. Don't pretend that the culture you are building is the only one available. Jesus came right out and acknowledged the way that the world's leaders led, but He offered an alternative. You can't activate the team towards the right culture if you don't acknowledge what it is you are building and how it differs from the norm.

- **Address**- We must unapologetically address what our team is building. Jesus came charging in and let the team know: "Guys, among us, we are doing something different!" We must not shy away from addressing and identifying the team culture. We must have a united language that builds up the team culture. Begin by saying, "Among us, it will be different!"

Unity is the Name of the Game

My husband and I have something we say quite often. It is "We are Team Aman."

We often refer to being "Team Aman" before any project we are about to do, or some hard challenge we are about to embark on. This motto was something we started early in our marriage (before kids), and now we are expanding our team by having children.

There is something so uniting about this simple declaration.

When the odds seem stacked against us, or the chore list is against us, we face the challenge as "Team Aman," and even the impossible feels possible. We are forging in our marriage and family that we are a united front, a team, and we face challenges and opportunities together.

Team unity happens through intentionality. Unity must be cultivated and guarded. Most sports movies have a fairly predictable moment where a group of talented athletes are all doing their own thing, trying to be their personal best. There is then open disunity among certain teammates and alliances form. Finally, there is a pivotal moment when the coach draws the line in the sand… He finally has enough and gives an epic speech to the team about unity, and takes drastic measures to ensure that unity happens, even at the risk of losing his star athlete. The movie typically ends with the team responding, the star coming into compliance, and a buzzer-beating championship moment!

I've seen more of these movies than I can count and I love this plot line every single time! If only we could all create a united team through one epic speech.

At our core we all know that unity is essential for the health and effectiveness of our teams. I believe we are aware that if we plan to be a successful leader, we must have a healthy united team.

The question isn't, "Should we do this?" but rather, "How do we do this?

How do we take a group of people and make them a team of people committed to the grander vision and mission?

A culture of unity begins with you, the leader.

Looking at the example of Nehemiah's leadership, we see that he was a team player before he ever led his own team. He faithfully served on the king's team and only left the palace to build the wall when the king was in unity with Nehemiah's plan.

The best "team builders" have learned to be the best "team players." You cannot model what you have not lived. In every season and situation we must work as leaders to be above reproach in the area of unity. Our teams need to see us being the greatest champions of unity on the team.

Tools to Cultivate a Culture of Team Unity

- **Honor the gifts represented on the team-** A team that compliments and recognizes the giftings of their fellow teammates is a team heading for success. A united team is not intimidated by the giftings of their team members. Instead they are quick to acknowledge and honor the skills and talents in others. The result is that the leader pulls the best out of each team member. (Pride cannot acknowledge another's strength. There is almost nothing more detrimental to a team than allowing prideful team members to remain if they refuse to change.) As leaders, let's be quick to call out and honor the gifts that are represented. Let's celebrate the unique abilities that each team member possesses and highlight how it helps the team. This is a powerful tool for cultivating a heart of unity among our teams.

- **Sound the alarm against disunity-** There are a lot of things on a team that you can live with. And while some issues take time to fester before it's time to take action, disunity is not one of them. Disunity demands the alarms to sound and immediate action to be taken. The same is true for division. Disunity and division spread rapidly, like an infection. Nehemiah knew there was potential for enemies to attack and divide his team. As a result, he implemented an alarm system so that the team could respond to acts of division quickly. In Chapter four, we get some insight as to how Nehemiah's team was to respond to an attack. *"And I said to the nobles and to the officials and to the rest of the people, "The work is great and widely spread, and we are separated on the wall, far from one another. In the place where you hear the sound of the trumpet, rally to us there. Our God will fight for us."* (Neh 4:19-20.)

When they heard the trumpet they were to come running and rally together. When enemies came, they agreed to fight together! We must teach our teams to rally together and equip them with tools that enable them to war against the enemies of disunity and division. We must teach our teams to run head-on towards the source of attack instead of hiding and pretending that the enemy doesn't exist. Remember, we defeat disunity through intentional rallying points of team unity!

- **Guard the team-** It's always amazing to me when watching a sporting event on tv and a questionable call is made by one of the referees. Immediately, the coach charges out to "passionately dispute" the call. At first glance, it seems like a major overreaction, and then I realize what he's doing. He's sending a major signal to his team that he has their back. As the coach he's willing to run out to their defense, even if it costs him his pride. Often, after this theatrical moment from the coach, his team will have a massive play or breakthrough. Why? They are freshly united because they feel guarded! I have seen it time and time again in my role as a leader. When the teams I lead know I have their back, they are far more productive than I could have imagined. Respect and loyalty are fueled in team members when they know their leader will do whatever it takes to guard and protect the team!

Coaching the Team for the Win!

The win starts in the heart of the leader.

You can have a united team ready to link arms and march wherever is needed, but it takes a leader to direct the unity towards a victory.

Engaged leaders are not sitting on the sidelines hoping the team can figure out their way. An engaged leader is actively invested in doing whatever it takes to win the game.

If you are going to effectively build what is in your heart to build, you have to have a fire in you that will not settle for anything less than a win. A few other words that come to my mind when I think of an engaged leader include:

Grit.

Passion.

Endurance.

Resilience.

Your team will be infused with these attributes to the degree that they are infused in you as their leader.

A united and passionate team is ready to be coached for the win.

People will leave everything on the field for a coach who is invested in winning the game. They will leave a lot behind to serve the vision of someone who is invested in paying the price to see that victory is achieved.

As leaders, it is our job to lead the team to victory. We don't have to sugarcoat the vision or prop the team up, but instead, take a united group and direct them towards the finish line. It's to be right beside them if they fall, cheering them onward when things get hard, and to keep pressing them to reach the goal. It is to be the voice beside them with affirmations and necessary declarations. Our job as leaders is to encourage our team and build them up so they don't lose their confidence.

A united team, with an engaged leader, has the potential to do the impossible.

Behind the curtains of every great victory, you will find a great coach who led the way. Behind the scenes of the victory lap, are many unglamorous moments when a coach spurred the team to push beyond their comfort zone and into a place they never thought possible.

Perhaps one of the greatest gifts we can give our teams is to keep talking. Keep leaning over the fence calling out their potential. It's to coach them and remind them of the goal each step of the way.

Somewhere along the journey of you coaching them for the win, you establish a team who believes the impossible is possible and that commitment and unity results in the win.

CHAPTER 10
IN THE TRENCHES WITH THEM

Lean Into the Here and Now: Be Present

One of the greatest schools of leadership is called motherhood. If you think you're an expert on how to activate a group towards a common goal and mission, just try and convince a toddler to do what you want them to do. You'll re-evaluate all of your leadership tactics after you try to get a small human to buy into what you're selling! Do you want to train for negotiating with a terrorist? Just convince a toddler why they need a bedtime.

Truly, my rookie season of parenting is teaching me so much about effectively leading and serving others. One of the biggest lessons I am slowly learning, and often failing at, is the power of being present! My son, Wesley, is often unimpressed with the toys and gifts we give him. He would much prefer having my husband and I present with him. He cries by the door when Daddy goes to work. He just wants to have Dad by his side to play, laugh, and give him all the snacks. Simply put, my son values his father's presence more than his "presents!"

I've discovered that my team feels the same way. One of the greatest gifts I can give them is to be present, here, and in the moment with them. People will often give their best to a leader who they know is with them, is personally invested in them, and present in the process of building. An investor simply offers money and often isn't even known by many who benefit from it. An effective leader must invest his life into that which he's building.

People follow leaders, not simply investors.

An engaged leader has their pulse on the future, and what is needed to continue to move the ball forward. But they are also deeply anchored in the present.

Great leaders are engaged with all that is happening right here and right now. Yes, someone needs to think about and plan for the future, but leading for the future alone is not enough. Those we are leading need to know that what they are doing today matters and that we are personally invested in that.

This is really, really hard.

I am the chiefest of offenders in the whole "not being present thing."

I am a visionary. I am a leader.

By the time I have innovated, motivated, and now stepped into the activation season, I am ready for the next big mountain. Often, at the very moment the team is activated to build, I am dreaming about the next thing we need to build. If I am not careful I can very quickly tear down the morale of the team by not being in the moment.

It takes intentionality to stop what I am doing, to stop looking ahead, and be fully present with what is being built by the team in the here and now.

In my opinion, one of the most moving accounts in the Bible is when Jesus heals the woman with the issue of blood. The whole scene leading up to the miracle is one of chaos because Jesus is in a hurry. He has somewhere important to go. Jesus is on His way to heal an influential man's daughter, so the situation is urgent.

On the way, there's a woman who is desperate, but not wanting to be an inconvenience, she decides to quickly touch Jesus' robe so she can be healed. She doesn't try to stop Jesus, instead she reaches out and touches the hem of His garment. In this story, Jesus shows us something completely counter-culture. He is in the middle of an important task, and yet, He stops, waits, and looks for the individual who touched His garment. Jesus asked, "Who touched me?" His disciples think He's crazy to try and figure out who touched Him in such a massive crowd! But Jesus was going to use the moment, because He cared for the individual more than anything else. This woman's body was physically healed, but Jesus would engage this woman and restore life and healing to her. Jesus was present in the here and now. Throughout His ministry, He always had time for the person right in front of Him.

Spoiler alert!! Even after delaying His journey and taking time to be present with this woman, Jesus went on to heal the man's daughter. Perhaps, in our leadership, being present with our team makes them feel like they win by being with us. And we still are able to accomplish the task that we originally set out to do.

How to Lean In and Be Present in the Here and Now:

- **Slow down-** Nothing screams "I don't care" louder than being rushed and distracted in the presence of our teams. EVERYTHING takes longer when you incorporate others. Like the old African Proverb says, *"If you want to go fast, go alone. If you want to go far, go together."* If you are going to activate the full potential out of your team, it takes time, and it takes slow time. Our lives have been greatly affected through the new tools afforded us via technology. I am a gadget nerd and love staying apprised of the newest time saving, efficiency-boosting tools. Yet, it doesn't take a rocket scientist to figure out some of these tools have become personal weapons when it comes to our engagement and interactions with our teams. These "time saving" tools have left us busier than ever and more disengaged from the present time than anyone could have imagined. How many times are we caught "multi-tasking," aka disengaged in the moment and rushing past the human right in front of us? We must slow down to be present in the moment and engaged with the person right in front of us. To slow down and engage with our teams, we must make intentional changes in our schedule, behaviors, and even body language. Perhaps you need to schedule appointments that are titled "Slow down and engage the team." Plan a time to go sit in a team meeting you don't normally sit in on. Leave your phone in the other room and simply walk around looking for someone on your team that you can encourage. Take an intentional look at your schedule and evaluate if you are moving faster than your team can actually go. Take a deep breath, slow down, and enjoy the right now with your team.

- **Listen intently-** Kids have a rather effective tactic of grabbing the full attention of their parents. A child will often grab the face of their parent with both hands and stare directly into their eyeballs while they talk. Now, you probably shouldn't attempt this tactic in your next staff meeting since it would create an awkward moment, to say the least. When you are in conversation, be fully present and really listen. Set the phone face down, put the devices away, lean forward, and look at your team member straight in the eye as you listen. Even your posture can send the signal of being fully present in the here and now with the person right in front of you. There is nothing more demoralizing than talking with someone who is constantly looking over your shoulder or looking down at their device. On the contrary, there is nothing quite so encouraging as when you engage in a conversation and the person on the other side is fully present and listening! Listening intently means not just listening when we deem it important. If it matters to the individual, it matters to me!

- **Cheer loudly-** The voice your team needs to hear the most is yours. There is nothing like hearing the sound of your family members and friends cheering for you on the sideline. You run faster, play better, and are far less tempted to quit because you know they are present. No one can build your team up as well as you can. They need to hear your voice encouraging them, coaching them, and letting them know they are not alone! There is a song from the movie, "The Bucket List" called "Say What You Need to Say." The lyrics keep repeating, "Say what you need to say," over and over again. As leaders, may we not hold back the words of affirmation and encouragement from our team, may we be the first and last voice they hear cheering them on!

They Will Follow Your Feet More Than Your Words

One of the worst pieces of advice is, "Do as I say not as I do."

You can say that until you're blue in the face but your team is watching your actions more than listening to your words.

I remember growing up knowing that Friday was always chore day in our home. Each of us kids and my parents had different tasks and responsibilities on this day. What I remember most though was the feeling that we were all in it together. It wasn't a one-man show, there weren't spectators with a few participants. Though our responsibilities were different, we were all in the trenches together! Suddenly, what could have felt overwhelming and lonely became a whole lot better because we knew we were all invested in the same mission. Operation "Make Mom Happy with a Clean House!"

People will commit to hard work and radical sacrifice when they know they are not alone. Many organizations are now creating workspaces that are more communal than ever before. The goal is to boost the morale and efficiency of the team. There is something so encouraging when you can look around the room and see that you're in it together, and no matter how long it takes, everyone is invested and committed to achieving the same goals.

Nehemiah was a man who was in the trenches with his team. He didn't ask them to pay a price he hadn't already paid, or was willing to pay. He didn't just invest in getting the vision, but he invested in building the vision.

How do you build a wall in fifty-two days under great opposition? One major way is having a leader on the front lines who is building, encouraging, coaching the serve, and showing with his actions what he wants from each member of the team.

We come to that moment in the building of the wall when the voice of the enemy is loud against the people. In that moment, we don't find Nehemiah in a strategy room. He's not sending out an email to his core leadership team. Instead, we find him stationed on the wall, building in the trenches.

"We worked early and late, from sunrise to sunset. And half the men were always on guard. I also told everyone living outside the walls to stay in Jerusalem.

That way they and their servants could help with guard duty at night and work during the day. During this time, none of us—not I, nor my relatives, nor my servants, nor the guards who were with me—ever took off our clothes. We carried our weapons with us at all times, even when we went for water." **Neh 4:21–23 (NLT)**

We must remember that the book of Nehemiah is written like a leadership diary. We are getting an insider's look at key moments of Nehemiah's leadership. There are a few key cultural pieces we observe in this recap from Nehemiah:

- **Communicate a culture of "We"-** Who is going to build the wall and continue to guard and protect it? We are. Nehemiah doesn't say that only he would work from sunrise to sunset. He doesn't say only the people would be busy, but he said, "We worked." The way we communicate culture is vital. It is either intentionally activating a team culture or it's tearing it down. People must be reminded that this is a "we" thing, not a me thing. They must see a leader who owns the wins and the losses. Team members appreciate a leader who says we are in this together when everything is peachy, and is just as invested when nothing seems to be going right.

- **Create a culture of all hands on deck-** Healthy teams are filled with activated participants, not disengaged spectators.

Nehemiah calls all hands to the deck. Those that were living outside the walls were asked to remain inside the walls for a season, long enough to help build and guard. As you are in the trenches of activation and building, you must create a culture of contribution and hard work. Nehemiah proved that he would work, and he was not afraid to set the bar high for full team participation. One of the greatest enemies of a healthy team culture is entitlement. Those who are entitled become a group of disengaged, badge-wearing team members. An active contributor does the work even without a title. Nehemiah had a team of leaders around him that weren't striving for a title but were there to help and contribute. Not only are you communicating a culture of "we," but you are creating a culture where everyone on the team helps carry the weight together!

- **Model the culture of devotion**- What is the best way to show somebody how you want them to build? Show them! Nehemiah 4:23 describes the kind of devoted leader that Nehemiah was and how his team was like-minded. *"During this time, none of us—not I, nor my relatives, nor my servants, nor the guards who were with me—ever took off our clothes. We carried our weapons with us at all times, even when we went for water."* Wow, he didn't even change his clothes in the heat of the battle or building. People don't need a bulletin posted on the wall describing commitment and hard work. They need a front-row seat to observe their leaders modeling a commitment to hard work. What you model, you can unashamedly ask others to do. The greatest billboard of the vision is you, the leader, side by side with your team showing them the way!

Remember, This is Big

Many of us need to stop singing, "Somewhere over the rainbow…" You probably just started humming the melody in your head, didn't you?

Somewhere and some day are the great enemies of right here, right now. One of the greatest gifts we can give those we lead is making sure they understand that "THIS IS BIG!" Right here, this task, this is significant. This meeting. This conversation. What we are building is big and it's where our heart is.

We need to be present and in the moment with our team, but also present in our hearts. We don't go from opportunity to opportunity, but from passion to passion, making the most of that which we are building, and feeling good about the process.

Trust and loyalty are forged in the hearts of your team when they know you believe in what you're building, and that you are happy to build alongside them.

It is a lie that "Somewhere else" or "Some day" matters more. The fruit of your leadership that you enjoy down the road, will be the product of the seeds you sowed in this season. In other words, the house you are building right now is the one that you will live in at some point in the future.

Just make sure you like the fruit of your current investment.

Here is how to make sure.

Make sure the journey of getting there is filled with joy and passion for your team. Most often the regrets of a leader are not that they engaged too much, but that they missed the moments that were right in front of them with those who were around them. Many leaders who have built something of significance didn't recognize the "significant" moments until after they happened. Success is often the product of showing up day after day, building with the same team, doing the same routines over and over. When you look back, you realize how big it was. Each day you engaged with the team and built alongside them. You built something of significance.

If you were to walk into the San Antonio Spurs locker room, you would find a quote posted in every language that the team speaks. It's a quote by the poet Jacob Riis: "*When nothing seems to help, I go and look at a stonecutter hammering away at his rock perhaps a hundred times without as much as a crack showing in it. Yet at the hundred and first blow it will split in two, and I know it was not that blow that did it -- but all that had gone before."*

Grab your hammer, saddle up next to your team, and make this moment count.

Every swing, every hit, every conversation, is worth it.

Which moment is big?

This one.

You never know, this moment might be the moment when you see the full fruit of that which you built. Together. Side by side. With those that matter most!

CHAPTER 11
KNOW THE STATE OF THE TEAM

Feedback is Your Friend

I was homeschooled for all but one month of my K-12 education years. I went to a private Christian school for one month in kindergarten, just long enough to warrant me getting a lunchbox and the students to throw me a going away party!

My mom was my primary teacher, along with my three siblings. (We are forever indebted to her for her patience and for not killing us!)

My mother is a woman of many words and loves all things that pertain to words.

Put a word game in front of her and she is a force to be reckoned with. This love of words caused her to have a keen interest in all of us kids learning to write, and to be on the straight and narrow when it came to our grammar.

In my teen years, I would turn in my self-perceived, beautifully typed, literary masterpiece to my mother. I would then have it handed back to me with the dreaded red ink. How could my mother do this to me? She would mark up my paper and notate every misplaced punctuation mark. She would also correct my spelling errors, and add her comments for change.

With each mark of red, I could feel my pride being challenged. Reluctantly, and with my head hung low, I would take the marked-up paper and return to the drawing board for round two.

My fourteen-year-old self couldn't recognize that the red pen marks were a beautiful gift from my mother. I misinterpreted feedback as rejection when in reality, it was a tool to help me achieve long-term success.

Since then I've learned that inviting the red pen of feedback into my life and leadership is essential for a culture of success.

We can instill in the hearts of our team a love for feedback and a hunger to invite the red pen into their lives! It's a gift to them.

As you've probably figured out by now, any piece of culture we want to embed into the fabric of our teams must first be evidenced in our own lives. A healthy culture of feedback and personal awareness must begin with us. To the degree I allow feedback from my team to me, is the degree my team will receive feedback from me. The way I respond to the red pen of input sets the tone for how my team responds.

Taking a piece of wisdom given to the sharks from the Pixar movie, "Finding Nemo." "Fish are friends, not food."

Feedback is your friend, not your enemy.

Feedback helps you measure the true state of your team. With it, you have an accurate pulse on the morale of your organization.

If we're honest, feedback can be terrifying.

It's easier to plug our ears and close our eyes to the messes on the team. Even the best leaders can adopt the childhood lie that if I close my eyes you can't see me. If I don't acknowledge the mess on my team, then it doesn't exist.

First, closing our eyes to the problem doesn't make it go away, but rather magnifies it. Second, ignoring problems within an organization causes the morale and heart of your team to deflate.

Being ignorant, or worse, rejecting honest feedback, is a big mistake. A widely perceived thought is that the red pen of correction is to be feared. In reality, what should invoke fear in the heart of a leader is when the team puts the pen away and becomes silent. The minute your team stops talking is the minute you know they've stopped caring.

Colin Powel, a retired four-star general in the United States Army, said this: *"The day the soldiers stop bringing you their problems is the day you stopped leading them. They have either lost confidence that you can help them or concluded that you do not care. Either case is a failure of leadership."*

Silence on the team speaks very loudly and it should be a grave concern to us as leaders.

Silence Can Mean a Few Things.

- You've lost their confidence.
- You've lost their trust.
- You've lost their passion.

The more I have led the more I recognize that when my team brings feedback and input, it means they are invested. Will there be times that your team shares their feedback at the worst moments? Absolutely. Will there be situations where the feedback they give is inaccurate or missing the pulse? One hundred percent.

Are the rewards of allowing feedback greater than the risks? Without a doubt!

I will take a team member who is willing to assess and give feedback any day over the person who sits silently on the team unengaged and distant from the heart of what is happening.

If we are going to accomplish the mission of building a God-sized vision, we must learn to fall in love with the red pen of feedback. If we are going to develop teams that are effective builders, we must create a culture where they crave feedback!

One study found that in a work context, *"69% of employees say they would work harder if they felt their efforts were better recognized."* Seven out of ten employees would be more activated simply by knowing that they are seen!

A culture of feedback is one where people know they are seen, valued, and worth being developed. We are wired for feedback and acknowledgment.

Silence isn't Always Golden-

Believe it or not, too much silence can drive you crazy. According to an article from the Smithsonian Magazine, *"The quietest place on earth, an anechoic chamber at Orfield Laboratories in Minnesota, is so quiet that the longest anybody has been able to bear it is 45 minutes."* This laboratory is used to primarily measure how loud a product is, but when a human sits in the dark silence of this room, it can begin to make them go mad!

I propose that a team environment where there is a silence of feedback in either direction causes teams to go crazy. Silence in an organization breeds fear, isolation, insecurity, and negative competition. People will begin to write their own narrative in the midst of silence in your organization.

You know you have lost someone's heart when you have lost their voice. When you see the team go silent, it's time to change the schedule and do whatever it takes to begin to engage the individual and find out where they are at.

As long as we are still talking, we can keep growing!

It is our responsibility as leaders to create an atmosphere that encourages and welcomes intentional feedback. We must create consistent, simple, and strategic pathways for feedback to happen on our teams. If we create opportunities for feedback at the highest level of leadership, our teams will begin to create that same culture among their teams.

A Few Practical Ways to Create Feedback Loops Among Your Team:

- **Create a metric of feedback that defines the win-**

  Identify and clarify a clear metric of what a win looks like on the team! It's hard to have a culture of healthy feedback if everyone's interpretation of the win looks different. When you clarify what the win is and how it will be measured, it helps the entire team be able to give and receive feedback!

- **Assess as a team as often as it happens-** Build into your team a culture of expectation for feedback, where everyone knows that after every event there is a feedback conversation. If it's a weekly event, then weekly assess it. If it happens once a year, then when it's finished, have a feedback meeting and make notes for the following year. Ideally, you would meet in person to have these feedback sessions, but if necessary, you can have digital meetings and even start the dialogue over text or email.

- **Set a feedback meeting with each individual on your team-** One of the biggest surprises to me in leading people is how much they desire genuine feedback on their personal performance. Most people feel insecure about their performance if it's never talked about. More often than not, they interpret the silence as an acknowledgment of their failure or shortcomings. A thirty-to sixty-minute one-on-one meeting with your team goes a long way. Prepare a few key questions that will generate dialogue with the team member, then listen to what they are saying! I have found in these meetings that people are often aware of where they are missing it. So you are providing a safe environment to hear them out and give constructive criticism. I have also found that when I just listen to the individual, some of the best ideas for the whole team emerge. Your members will cherish these opportunities for feedback if you create a space for them to happen!

● **Create a culture of "If you correct it, you must be committed to correct it!"**- It is important to create a culture on the team that is committed to not just seeing the problem but becoming part of the solution. Healthy feedback is not a "complain session," or "tear down the team time!" We want feedback on what's not working or how things can get better, but we also want a team of people who are committed to following through the whole process of seeing the issue resolved. If someone is going to give feedback on how it can get better, they need to come to the table with an idea of how this can happen. This creates a culture where everyone knows that each member is committed to the success of the team, not just declaring what's wrong with it! The person who sees the area that needs improvement usually has the capacity to solve the problem if they commit to helping.

- **Everyone talks: Repeat back what you think you hear**- A healthy team is one where there is full group participation. People can all appear to be on the same page and understand the conversation, but if you never hear them verbalize what they are hearing, then how do you know? After something has been communicated to the team, it's important to create the opportunity for members to repeat back to you what they heard. I have been in too many meetings where the leader thought they communicated well, but later learned there was miscommunication. When there is time for the team to repeat back what they are hearing, you know if you are communicating clearly and if everyone is on the same page. This practice goes both ways. We can often misinterpret what our teams are communicating to us. A lot would be clarified if we repeated back what we are hearing. This tells the team that we hear them, we value their input, and are committed to being on the same page!

The more we create pathways for honest and healthy feedback, the more the hallways become filled with the beautiful sound of laughter and dialogue. In the silence, we can lose the hearts of our team, but in the conversation, passion and joy arise.

Don't be Tone Deaf

I have a love-hate relationship with music.

Obviously, I'm a musician.

You see, in the eyes, or should I say the ears, of a musician, there is no such thing as "background music." If there is any form of a melody or beat being played, the attention of the musician is taken away. We critique and note every layer and track that's being played. Every nuance and melodic addition hidden in the track is like an Easter egg hunt for us music nerds. Suddenly, our vocabulary changes when we start dissecting a song. We say things like, "Those vocals are like butter" or "That groove is in the pocket." If I am texting my older brother, Jake, about a song, we rate it on whether or not it's "a speed skate" worthy song. You know, the Celine Dion song that no one admits to liking as a kid, but when it came on at the Roller Odyssey, you started speed skating like nobody's business!

Back to why I have a love-hate relationship with music. When the music is interesting and good, I love it. When it's terrible, off-key, and lacks rhythm, it's like someone is repeatedly stabbing my eardrums!

It never ceases to amaze me how many people are convinced of their musical grandeur, while they couldn't find the right key if they tried. They sing with gusto while being completely unaware that they are tone-deaf.

If that's you, please don't let me discourage you from singing your guts out in the shower. Just please hand the microphone back!

If you want to find where many of these tone-challenged people are, take a cruise. I am guilty of having spent hours of my time on a cruise ship watching people sing karaoke. There always seems to be a group of the same people who keep getting up under the light show and belting out their favorite seventies ballad and eighties rocker song! One cruise I went on, a woman brought a CD carrier with her own karaoke background tracks! Now that's dedication! As a musician, I am flabbergasted as I watch these passionate people sing completely unaware of their surroundings and unconcerned that they are butchering these once musical masterpieces.

If we are honest, we can be guilty of the above when it comes to our leadership. We can be completely tone-deaf to what our team and situations are communicating all around us. As a leader, I have had my fair share of times where I looked more like the karaoke singer concentrating so hard on the screen making sure I sang the written words, that I forgot to check if I was in the correct key!

Leading and building effectively requires keen awareness and perceptiveness to what is happening all around us. It requires intentionality to listen to every word and the layers of tone that are being communicated from our teams.

As leaders, we must fight against the tendency to be tone-deaf to what our teams, organizations, and spreadsheets are telling us. Passion alone isn't enough. You can passionately miss knowing where your team and organization is actually standing.

Nehemiah was keenly aware of the state of his team, and the tone they were using when speaking. There comes a point in building the wall when real enemies and voices of discouragement want to lead the builders astray. Nehemiah didn't just pretend that everything was rosy. He didn't ignore the problem. Instead, he dealt with it head-on.

Sanballat and Tobias kept coming to discourage Nehemiah and the people. But in addition to that, multiple voices were inviting the people to leave the work. In fact, ten different times voices went to the people and said, "Return to us." Here is a pivotal moment in how Nehemiah will handle this. He can turn the speaker up so he doesn't hear the fears of the people, or he can directly speak into the heart of the situation and lead them through it.

In Nehemiah chapter 4:13-14, we see how he handles the situation based on his awareness of the state of his team.

"So in the lowest parts of the space behind the wall, in open places, I stationed the people by their clans, with their swords, their spears, and their bows. And I looked and arose and said to the nobles and to the officials and to the rest of the people, "Do not be afraid of them. Remember the Lord, who is great and awesome, and fight for your brothers, your sons, your daughters, your wives, and your homes." (ESV)

Nehemiah has his finger on the pulse of his team. He knows where they are, he acknowledges that there is a real threat, and then reminds them of the bigger picture!

Here are Some Tools to Help Us Lead Tuned In versus Tone-Deaf:

- **Acknowledge the elephant-** People see the elephant even if they don't acknowledge it. But beware of losing the trust of your team because you are unwilling to point out the elephant! Before you can refocus the team towards building, you have to look into their eyes and let your team know you see the same threat or problem they see. Admitting there is an elephant doesn't equal failure, it spurs hope in your team that you are committed to doing something about getting rid of it! People need to hear you vocalize your concern regarding the elephant, and that you are committed to doing something about it. Nehemiah coming forward and beginning to station people strategically while equipping them with tools was an acknowledgment to the team that he was fully aware of the alarm being sounded!

- **Hit it head on-** There might be an elephant in the room, but by golly, we aren't going to live with it. The moment you identify the concern, problem, or broken area, your team needs to see you leading them straight towards the fix! There are multiple ways to approach a problem, but the most effective is hitting it head on! Run fast, run hard, and run straight towards the mouth of the lion. Nehemiah wasted no time hitting the threat head on. He began to get weapons in the hands of the team and he strategically placed people to wage war against the problem. A healthy culture of feedback requires movement. It requires commitment to building correctly, bringing all threats to the surface, running towards an issue full speed ahead.

- **Remind them of the why-** In the middle of conflict or trying situations, remind your team of the mission. Nehemiah reminds the people of how awesome God was, and he reminds them of who they are fighting for. Nehemiah reminds them that it's for their sons, daughters, spouses, family, and homes. While being aware of what your team needs, you must also help keep them aware of why you are here in the first place. We must remember to not get so caught up in fighting alligators that our original goal was to drain the swamp. Many situations will face us and our teams that can cause us to forget our original mission. It is our job to lead people through the storm towards the same destination we were always meant to go.

Celebrate Throughout the Journey

What you celebrate will be repeated!

Those we lead watch closely to what is applauded and celebrated.

Every group that goes on the same road trip by vehicle has the same exact amount of miles to travel on their expedition. Yet, not every group has the same experience. One vehicle is filled with laughter, great tunes, and mass amounts of junk food! The other vehicle can be headed out in silence, with just carrot sticks for snacks, and some angry people listening to bad music. Both are on the same journey, but how they journey, and the way they arrive at the final destination is very different.

As leaders, we must determine how we want the journey to be for our teams. What if you arrive at the end goal very fast, but your whole team despises you, and life has been sucked out of the room? There are a lot of people on the journey to build something, but the spirit and culture by which they build makes all the difference.

Only you as a leader can determine how you want your team to feel on the journey. Will you create a culture of celebration, life, and joy? Will your method give them confidence that they can get there from here?

I want to lead people effectively to the end goal. I want them to arrive with hearts full of joy and laughter. It is possible to celebrate in the trenches, to laugh through the struggle, and encourage when doing the impossible.

CHAPTER 12
ENGAGE THE MISSION

Engage Now

Are you ready? That's good, but there are some things in life that no matter how prepared you are, you are never prepared enough. Marriage, children, new careers, pioneering something new, leadership, and the list goes on.

I remember returning home from our honeymoon and coming into our condo for the first time as Mr. and Mrs. Aman! I walked into our living room and sat in silence looking like I had just received the worst news in the world.

My new husband is looking at me as tears are about to billow forth. He proceeds to check on me to see if I'm ok, and I began to rapidly spew out with tears,

"I'm responsible for the atmosphere for our home!"

I'm sure at this moment Riley is saying to himself, " Who did I marry? She's crazy."

I'm a notorious over-thinker and visionary. Instead of embracing the moment and enjoying it, I was already worried that I hadn't properly prepared for this new responsibility of wifehood!

Tears poured from my eyes as I worried that I would set a terrible home atmosphere, I would utterly fail, and be a massive disappointment.

My husband graciously listened to my rant and fears, and then gently talked me off the ledge giving me an encouraging motivational speech! The truth was, I was on the verge of feeling paralyzed as I stepped in to engage this new season because I didn't feel prepared or qualified.

Anything worth giving yourself to and investing in rarely comes with feeling ready for it. It always requires an intentional decision to dive headfirst in and engage the work.

Throughout this book, we've looked at the necessity of engaged leaders. The process of leadership innovation, motivation, and activation. Now the ball is in your court and the clock is ticking. There is no time like the present.

The here and now to embrace the great work of building lays before you.

What You Do Have

It is so easy to look at all the things we don't have when it comes to our leadership abilities.

Yet, the real question is, "What do you have?" What abilities, resources, relationships, and vision do you have? It may not look like much, but even in the little something great can be forged and built.

I find there are two big "I don't have" excuses that can keep us from engaging leadership and building.

- I don't have the time
- I don't have what it takes

Excuse #1- I don't have the time

If you are waiting for the opportune time and the perfect moment, it's not coming. Now is the moment. Today is the day to press past fear and doubt and begin to engage the God-sized vision He has placed within you.

As I write these words I am a full-time, working mom with a new baby girl and a toddler. Plus, our world is in the middle of a pandemic. Nothing about now "feels" like the right moment or a convenient time. Yet, I know that I must continue forward, that what is being built is far greater than the circumstances or the feelings I have about it.

I don't want to look back in one, five, fifteen, or fifty years and wish I would have started building. I don't want to live in the fantasy land of "Some Day I Will."

Why not begin to build now?

It may be slow, it may be difficult, it may not look like much, but it's worth engaging in the here and now.

How do you build a cathedral? One brick at a time. How did Nehemiah build a wall in fifty-two days? By simply getting started!

Each one of us is given the same amount of minutes, hours, and days in a year. We all have about the same amount of heartbeats daily telling us that life continues. The question then is how will we use those minutes, hours, and days? Will we lean into each heartbeat and let them remind us that there is life coursing through our veins and there's plenty of opportunities to make each beat count?

What could happen if you chose to use the time you have to begin building with? Giving thirty minutes a day to engage your leadership may feel insignificant, but multiply that over a year and you'll have invested one-hundred-eighty-two and a half hours, or four weeks of full-time work into your leadership! Suddenly what feels like a small investment each day has the potential for an incalculable effect.

I implore you to decide to give energy each day to engage your leadership. Don't wait for another day or season, but begin investing in now with what is in front of you to build. Please don't minimize the time you have. Instead maximize it!

Excuse #2- I don't have what it takes

One snare or excuse that keeps us from engaging is believing that we don't have what it takes to succeed. If you gather a group of people and ask them to share their personal strengths or abilities, you'll often find a whole lot of eyeballs staring back at a loss as to what their abilities are.

We often undervalue or underestimate the skill sets we have, which means we miss their hidden potential and ability. And worse, start to look at other people's talents and skills and feel that we lack in comparison.

Anyone can make a list of things they can't do, but it takes a visionary to see the gifts people have and begin to build with that.

Sometimes you have to put into play the abilities you have and while using them, give energy to developing and acquiring more of the necessary tools.

Michael Jordan, arguably the greatest basketball player of all times said this regarding why he saw so much success in his career, *"I have missed more than 9,000 shots in my career. I have lost almost 300 games. On 26 occasions I have been entrusted to take the game-winning shot, and I missed. I have failed over and over and over again in my life. And <u>that is why I succeed</u>."*

Until you're willing to use what you have and willing to risk failing, you'll never succeed. The majority of people look at the need and ask themselves, "What if I fail?" The visionary looks around and asks, "What if I succeed?"

Stop what you're doing right now and write down ten things you currently have that can help you build and expand your leadership. Begin to identify and activate the tools that are currently around you and available to you.

If You Don't Have It, Build It

Innovation often begins when a leader sees something lacking, realizes that no one is fixing it, and gets to work building what no one else sees.

This was the kind of leader that Nehemiah was.

He saw the need for someone to rise up and build the wall. He didn't let lack keep him from building. Instead, he saw lack as an opportunity to build what didn't exist.

We've talked a lot about Nehemiah's leadership qualities in building the wall and governing the people. He truly was an incredible leader.

Something strikes me, though, regarding Nehemiah and reveals a potential greater depth to his character as a leader.

You see, there is a high probability that Nehemiah was a eunuch. The reason this may be true is because Nehemiah was an exile. Often, when new rulers came into power, they would castrate exiles who served in the king's palace, and especially if they were to serve around the queen.

If this is true, Nehemiah would never be able to be married and have children. Therefore, he would be deprived of having a physical legacy, and his name would not be carried on into future generations.

Yet, Nehemiah had an amazing legacy he left behind. He built what he didn't have. He had a far-reaching legacy that he built into others.

Nehemiah restored safety and a place of worship for the people of God. He ruled the land for twelve years and modeled to many people sacrificial leadership.

This is what it's all about. To pay the price for building something that outlasts us all: to invest in that which we don't currently see.

We have no record of Nehemiah having a wife or kids, but he invested so deeply in the families all around him.

As leaders, we don't just build something that will benefit us, but we build that which will serve those all around us, and leave a legacy that will last far beyond our lifetime.

Nehemiah may have not had heirs to carry his name on, but he built something that thousands of years later we are still talking about.

That's what I call legacy!

Sing Your Swan Song

Behold the swan.

The swan song has been talked about throughout ancient Greek culture literature and from the likes of Socrates, Aristotle, Plato, and more. The legend is that the mute swan is mostly silent throughout the duration of its life. In the last moments and breath of life, the swan begins to sing out the most beautiful melody and song. This swan waits until its final minutes to let out its most impacting sound. Right before dying, the swan finally releases the song that has been locked inside its whole life.

This legend is very sad to me. To think that an entire life can be lived without sharing something so beautiful to the world is tragic.

Within each of us is a swan song: Something of beauty and power that could bless and change the world around us.

What if we didn't wait until our dying breath to sing this song, but rather used all of our breaths until our dying breath to sing our swan song?

What if we refused to allow our swan song to remain dormant, and risked everything to begin to awaken it in this time and space?

Perhaps, you didn't realize it, but you have a song to be sung and a masterpiece to be created. The swan song is now often used in reference to an artist's final painting, or a musician's final song, or a writer's final chapter.

Why not change this? Why not begin to discover the beautiful masterpiece God created you to create and begin to build it in the here and now?

Think about the impact that we could have on the world around us if all of us refused to be silent, if we refused to wait until tomorrow, and began singing the song today!

May I propose that the cost of you not singing your swan song now is far greater than you can imagine. The swan whose last dying breaths is their song lets out a glorious melody but it dies with them. The leader who is willing to boldly sing their song now, not only has a beautiful melody that is heard, but a lifetime to teach others that which they have sung.

Sure, you might hit some sour notes. You may be shaking in your boots with fear as to how others will receive this masterpiece. But then again, you may find a whole army circling around you and joining you in the mission to sing the song that has been put inside of you.

Whatever you do, don't let the vision die inside of you.

Stay silent no more. Sing!

Punch fear in the face and start running boldly towards the God-sized vision that's on the inside of you.

You'll never know the impact you could have until you let the song come out of you!

Ready... Set... Engage!

ENDNOTES

CHAPTER 1
We Bought a Zoo, Directed by Cameron Crowe, 20th Century Fox, 2011

CHAPTER 2B
https://www.merriam-webster.com/dictionary/innovation
https://www.merriam-webster.com/dictionary/innovate

CHAPTER 3
Lewis, C.S, The Great Divorce, 1945.

CHAPTER 4
www.desiringgod.org/messages/george-muellers-strategy-for-showing-god

CHAPTER 5
Seth Godin,
https://seths.blog/2011/12/no-one-ever-bought-anything-in-an-elevator/
https://magicguides.com/disneyland-crowd-calendar/

CHAPTER 5B
www.merriam-webster.com/dictionary/motive
https://www.merriam-webster.com/dictionary/motivate
https://spaceflightnow.com/2020/03/15/spacex-launch-aborted-in-final-second-before-liftoff/

CHAPTER 7
This quote is originally attributed to best selling author John C. Maxwell.

CHAPTER 8
Patrick Lencioni from the Table Group at the 2012 Global Leadership Summit.

CHAPTER 8B
https://www.merriam-webster.com/dictionary/active
https://www.merriam-webster.com/dictionary/activate

CHAPTER 10
An unattributed African Proverb.

CHAPTER 11

Four-star general in the United States Army, Colin Powell.

https://officevibe.com/blog/infographic-employee-feedback
https://www.smithsonianmag.com/smart-news/earths-quietest-place-will-dri
ve-you-crazy-in-45-minutes-180948160/

CHAPTER 12

https://www.lifehack.org/articles/productivity/15-highly-successful-people-
who-failed-their-way-success.html

ACKNOWLEDGMENTS

They say it "takes a village" to raise a child, and I would argue it is the same to write a book! There are some key people who helped make this book a reality.

First I want to say a huge thank you to my husband Riley who has cheered me on from day one and been my number one cheerleader through not only the process of writing, but in my leadership journey!

I want to say a thank you to my three brothers, Jacob, Geno and Johnny! Each one of them has coached and encouraged me in this process of writing. I value their different leadership perspectives and their honest input to make me a more effective leader! Also a big thanks to my sister-in-laws Bethany and Ali for their feedback and encouragement throughout this journey.

I wouldn't be the woman or leader that I am without the love, affirmation, and coaching that my parents have given to me. They are my hero's and embody what it means to be an engaged leader! Thanks for letting me sit and cry as I read some of the first chapters of this book for you guys!

This book has been greatly enhanced because of the incredible editing skills of my dear friend Jamee Rae Pineda! Thank you for coaching me through the process and helping me truly communicate my voice and heart in this book! Also, a huge thank you to Pete Miller for helping with final edits!

Thank you to so many friends who have been cheering me on throughout this process and to my home Church, Joy, for helping me learn and grow on this journey of engaging leadership!

Lastly, I am forever grateful to my Lord and Savior Jesus Christ. I am humbled that He would save me, invite me on the journey of being His disciple, and give me the honor of getting to lead His people. I pray that everyday I would follow His example of leading through serving and shine His light wherever I go!

ABOUT THE AUTHOR

Natalie Aman is passionate about seeing the local Church grow, leaders equipped, and people stepping into their God given purpose! She has worked with youth and young adults for over 12 years and is now the Executive Pastor at Joy Church Medford. She also enjoys traveling to churches and conferences helping equip leaders and their teams. She has her Bachelors in theology from Vision International University. Natalie is married to Riley Aman and they have two amazing kids, Wesley and Annie! You can likely find Natalie at a local coffee shop throughout the week getting a nice cup of Joe!

If you're interested in having Natalie speak at an upcoming event or want more tools to help your team and you visit:

natalieaman.com

Made in the USA
Monee, IL
28 November 2020